MW00649385

A Page in History

A Page in History

Joe Kippley

ISBN: 1-57579-344-X

Library of Congress Control Number: 2006936155

Printed in the United States of America

PINE HILL PRESS
4000 West 57th Street
Sioux Falls, SD 57106

For my family and my U.S. Senate page family

TABLE OF CONTENTS

Introduction by Senator Tom Daschle

Afterword: A Generation's Challenge

Introduction

During my 26 years on Capitol Hill, I got to know hundreds of people working behind-the-scenes to ensure that our Senators and members of Congress could do the jobs they were elected to do. Some had been toiling in those halls for decades providing the institutional knowledge as members came and went. Some were young, just learning the ropes and eager to make a difference.

But one group of these "unsung heroes" always reminded me of why it was I was there – the pages. Sixteen-year old kids from across the United States who left their high schools, their families and friends and their normal teenage lives to come to Washington and serve their country side-by-side some of the most powerful men and women in the nation.

Their work ethic, stamina, professionalism and passion, especially at such a young age, always impressed and inspired me and my colleagues.

By the time the Senate-day started, the pages had already been to school in order to keep up with their classmates back home. They prepared the Senate chamber, making sure any bills or other documents, our charts and local newspapers were an arms-reach away. The pages always knew what was being debated on the floor and when a vote was expected, even when some of us Senators didn't! And they stayed on duty for as long as the Senate was in session, often late into the night.

Their duties were, and remain today, essential to the smooth operation of the United States Senate and House.

Joe Kippley and the other pages serving the Senate on September 11, 2001, and during the months immediately following had an experience unlike any other page class.

Most of these pages had been in Washington only a week the day of the attacks. They were just learning to navigate the corridors of the Capitol when they ran out of the building that morning. Not only were they adjusting to a new city, a new job and new friends, but there was an additional pressure after that morning – they were part of an institution our country and our world was looking to for guidance.

Memory should not dull the courage that was required of these young men and women. The Capitol was to have been the target for United Flight 93, which ultimately crashed in Pennsylvania. No one knew what was coming next. And yet these teenagers, many of whom were living away from home for the very first time, found the courage to come to work every day.

Those concerns must have been sharpened only 34 days later, when they, like all of us, were faced with a new fear when my office was the victim of an anthrax attack.

Despite these new dangers, the pages continued their work in Congress just like the rest of us. They didn't hide or shy away from their tasks. They were flexible as we all changed our daily routines. With courage and faith, they helped me and my colleagues labor through those difficult days. And they did it with a humor and exuberance that lifted many of our spirits.

All page classes are witnesses to historical events during their tenure, but this page class had a unique perspective on an event that changed our nation. It did not deter them from their duties nor dampen their spirits. Each of them has a remarkable story to tell, and I'm grateful that Joe Kippley is telling his.

It is my hope that their time with us in the Senate taught them not only of the risks that face those who serve their country, but of the tremendous potential for doing good. And I hope that the courage they showed during those difficult days in the fall of 2001 guides them back into public service so that their extraordinary talents and character can renew our democracy and strengthen it for the challenges to come.

–Senator Tom Daschle

Chapter 1
A Page in History

Surreal.

Moments ago it had been an average morning, but now I found myself running for my life. A Capitol Police officer had just informed everyone in the Senate Democratic cloakroom to evacuate "right away." The plain urgency of these words was enough to get my feet moving. I made it out of the cloakroom and down a set of marble stairs to the first floor along with the other Senate pages.

I planted my right foot firmly on the main floor and pushed off toward the north entrance of the Capitol. Another Capitol Police officer watched us round the turn as he played the role of the third base coach waving his runners home. He pointed to the exit with his left hand and wound his right arm quickly, as if I were the winning run. He may have yelled something to us as we evacuated, but I didn't hear him; his actions spoke loudly enough.

I had twenty yards to the doors as I passed the officer, and time started to slow. The new sense of urgency from this officer made me run faster, but the exit still could not come soon enough. Ahead stood a set of metal detectors, formerly a symbol of security and safety, but now obsolete since no one was trying to get into the building. There were plenty trying to get out, though. Senators and Representatives. Staffers and government officials. And Senate pages.

With ten yards to go, the unavoidable question crossed my mind. Would we make it out? Anyone thinking rationally would cite the astronomical odds of a plane striking the Capitol at the exact moment when I only had two or three seconds before I was out the northern end of the building. However, adrenaline and fear from the urgent call for evacuation overcame any sense of rationality.

With only a few feet between me and the exit, time slowed even further. Some pages in front of me had opened the doors and made their escape, and now I could see the light at the end of the tunnel. The sunlight of the beautiful morning reflected brightly outside off the white government buildings. While watching some of my friends move down the stairs outside, I reached forward with both arms and prepared to give the door a solid push to clear the way for myself and a couple of others following close behind me.

As I crossed the plane of the doorframe, time seemed to stop completely. My heart skipped a beat. I felt a sharp pain in my chest as I tried to take in a breath. I could tell that this stride was longer than my others; I was almost jumping past the exit way. I felt like a movie star in an action film where the building explodes just as the hero gets out. The short breath and sharp pain came from an actual expectation that the building would explode behind me. I felt a small smile come over my face for a moment, in part because I had caught my breath and in part because the building hadn't, in fact, exploded. Of course, rationality had gone out the door before I had, and I was only a 16-year-old kid a thousand miles from my home in South Dakota starting my second week of work as a Senate page.

Looking to the southwest, I could see smoke coming from the Pentagon. That is when the situation began to move from surreal to real. My eyes followed the smoke up to the blue sky, where I saw a plane that must have been trying to land at one of the Washington airports. It was too high and not headed in the right direction to be an immediate threat to the Capitol, but I had just seen planes turned into weapons on a television in the cloakroom, and I couldn't help but be slightly frightened by one in the sky directly above me.

Time raced back to its normal pace as I took the stairs two at a time and headed northeast toward the Russell Building and, ultimately, Webster Hall, the pages' home away from home. Eight of us gathered with the simple objective of making it back to our dormitory. The objective may have been straightforward, but the circumstances would make the journey complicated. First, we had only been in Washington a week, and we had always come to the Capitol through the Hart Building's underground tram system instead of directly from our dorm. Second, some members of this group had been overwhelmed by the emotions of the situation, and it was too much for them to bear. While I tried to gather my bearings to help guide the group back home, a couple of the girls began sobbing. They cried that they wanted to go home, and their pleas were filled with simple sincerity, as if they believed three clicks of their heels might take them back.

One of the guys in the group confirmed to me that we were headed in the right direction, so I became more confident that we would find our way back without much more trouble. I looked behind me to see if I could console any of the girls who were crying, but I saw that they were pretty shell-shocked. I didn't know any of these kids very well yet, so I didn't feel any words of comfort from me would carry much weight. We would all get a chance to call our families when we made it back to our dormitory. Maybe that would help calm us all down a bit.

When we reached Webster Hall, named after the Massachusetts Senator Daniel Webster, our first instruction was to go down to the basement and call home. I was one of the first to pick up a phone. I dialed the number quickly and waited for my mom to answer the phone. When she answered, I didn't really know what to say. I heard her voice, and I could feel myself crumble. I had not had any time to think about my fear until this moment. I had been acting out of adrenaline and instinct, but I began to think about my own well-being when I heard the voice of a person who was concerned about nothing else but that well-being.

"Hey, Mom. Just calling to say that I'm OK, and we evacuated the Capitol," I said after I had gathered some courage.

"OK, good. I've been watching the news here at home this morning," she said, so I guessed she probably knew more than I did.

I looked behind me and saw a handful of other pages eager to test their own mettle by calling their own families. "Mom, I need to let these other guys use the phone," I stammered with the feeling of a frog climbing up my throat and water welling in my eyes.

"Of course. Just call again when you get a chance," she said reassuringly.

I was fairly confident that I had sounded as strong as I could on the phone to reassure my mother, and she did a good job of acting as well.

Now there was nothing but time. Time to watch the television screens. Time to think about how in the world this average morning had turned into a time to run. I looked around and saw a common trait in many of my fellow pages—watery eyes. Tears fell from our eyes as we saw the Twin Towers crumble that morning on the television, but those tears were replaced by steel later that day when we were asked to come back to work on September 12th. We would be a part of a nation and its government moving forward to take on terrorism, and it would be our generation that would have to win this new war.

When I woke up on that average morning, I was just a 16-year-old kid, but I began to realize that I would be growing up a lot in the hours, days, weeks, and months ahead. I would be growing up in an historic time that would test the nation's will and spirit, as well as my own.

I was a page in history.

Chapter 2
Becoming a U.S. Senate Page

Aweek and a half earlier, I had arrived in Washington for only the second time in my life. I had visited two years before on a family vacation, but this would be an extended stay. On my first visit to Washington, my family had received a tour of the Capitol from a member of South Dakota Democratic Senator Tom Daschle's staff. The Senate was on a summer recess, so the floor was open.

Our guide described the Senate chamber and told some of its gloried history. All of this was interesting, but only one thing from that tour sticks with me to this day. Our guide pointed to the steps of the rostrum leading up to the presiding officer's chair and said, "This is where the pages sit."

"Wow," I thought to myself after she explained what pages were, "that would be the best job in the world!"

I learned that one could serve as a Senate page while in the junior year of high school, which was only a couple of years away for me at the time. The seed was planted in my mind, and it began to come to life less than a year later when I visited Senator Daschle's website. I printed the necessary information to begin an application through Daschle.

Like a snowball down a hill, the application process took off, accumulating many layers throughout the spring and summer of 2001. I sent a letter of interest, along with some other paperwork, to Daschle and received a positive response. I reached out to former teachers and community leaders to write letters of recommendation for me. A Daschle staffer then contacted me to set up a phone interview with Daschle's office manager. Even though I had set out with humble intentions, I now had a group of loyal family and friends rooting for me to get this job, and there was no backing down.

The phone rang one morning that summer at the appointed hour, and I took a deep breath before answering. I knew that I had what it took to get the job as a Senate page, so I calmed myself down with a thought that would help me far beyond this one phone call: "If God has a purpose for me to get this job and gain this experience, He will help me through."

The first question from that phone interview was harder than it sounded: "Tell me about yourself." Well, first, it wasn't even a question. I had my résumé in front of me, and I ticked off a few facts, but I wasn't entirely confident that what I said was what the interviewer wanted to hear. I soon found a comfort zone in the interview format where I could express my desire to serve the U.S. Senate with a true passion for our government. I hung up the phone knowing that I had made my case for being appointed to the U.S Senate Page Program.

By now my close friends, along with all of my extended family, knew that I was waiting on one phone call that would inform me of my status as a page, or lack thereof. That phone call came, fittingly enough, at a family reunion that summer. I took the call in a room with my father and his six brothers. I gave Dad the thumbs-up as I was offered the position, and he answered back with a thumbs-up and a beaming smile of pride. I quickly accepted the job and settled in to await further information on the program.

My uncles love to make fun of each other, and my dad gets his fair share of good-natured ribbing. After congratulating me on my upcoming job, they would point to my dad and ask snidely if I was really the son of "that guy." I would just laugh, and then laugh again as my dad joined in the jesting with self-deprecating humor. Of course, it was all in good fun, and it lifted the spirit of the whole family. Both of my paternal grandparents had passed away in the last decade, but I could sense their pride through my dad.

Phone calls were quickly made to inform my mother and her side of the family. My parents have been divorced since I was in third grade. I won't pretend that it was an easy experience, but I don't question God's wisdom because, since the divorce, I have observed first-hand that life has a way of working out. My mom remarried, and my step-dad has been great. The experience made me stronger in the long run, and now I have three loving parents instead of two. It strengthened my faith to find that a bad situation could turn out well even with most of the events out of my control. The divorce also taught me that the family structure is a valuable foundation for individuals, along with society as a whole, and shouldn't be taken lightly.

My entire family supported me as I prepared for this experience, and my dad planned to join me on my second journey to Washington. I would come home only for Thanksgiving and Christmas, and at the end of the semester-long program in mid-January. The period from September to Thanksgiving would be the longest I had ever been away from home. It would have taken only a handful of days to break my previous record, but this would be nearly three months.

I said goodbye to my step-dad with a handshake and a smile, and then turned to my mom. She was the weaker of the two of us at this goodbye, but she would prove to be the stronger when saying hello on September 11th. She cried a bit while I tried to reassure her that my time as a page would go by quickly, but at just 16 years old, I was her first child to leave home for such a lengthy period. I gave her a hug and walked out the door with my dad. The emotion hit me then as I walked to the car on the chilly morning; it was as if I knew I would need my mother in the coming weeks, but she wouldn't be there.

My dad and I drove to the airport and landed in Washington later that day. He got me pumped up for the new program and encouraged me to try to meet the other pages quickly and make plenty of friends. I surged with confidence with my dad at my side.

We rolled up to Webster Hall and began the registration process. I began to meet the other pages and their parents. I ended up being one of the last pages to arrive, so some others were already getting to know each other when I arrived. I stuck close to my dad for the most part and interacted mainly with my roommates. All the rooms were designed for four people with two sets of bunk beds. I would grow especially close to my roommates Adam Anthony, Jay Wright, and Vic Bailey. They were southern gentlemen from Virginia, Alabama, and South Carolina, respectively. My dad helped me get settled in my room on the second floor, and then the parents joined the new page class on an orientation visit to the U.S. Senate.

It was Sunday, September 2nd, when I entered the Senate chamber for the second time in my life. I looked around at my new place of work and couldn't believe it. The setting would become even more incredible when the Senate came into session that Tuesday and Senators milled about on the floor in front of me.

Then-Majority Leader Tom Daschle had appointed me, so I was a Democratic page. I served the full U.S. Senate, but I sat on the Democratic side of the rostrum and reported to the Democratic cloakroom. For the first time in my life, I was a Democrat. Well, technically I was too young to register to vote as a member of any party, but I had always considered myself a Republican. Fortunately, there was no problem with this, and there were cases on the other side of the aisle where Republican pages considered themselves Democrats personally.

I was born in Reagan's landslide year of 1984 and grew up siding with the Bush, Dole, and Bush campaigns for the presidency. I found the conservative values of the Republican Party to be most in line with my personal beliefs, but at the same time I admired the work of a fellow South Dakotan who could rise to the level of majority leader. Many people asked me before, during, and after the page program how I could work for the Democrats and Tom Daschle. I honestly believed that working for the Democrats was a blessing going into the program. I was too young to get completely stuck in my conservative Republican ways, and it was good for me to work with and for people with ideas different from my own. I learned that Democrats have many great ideas, and I learned how to respectfully disagree with their philosophy. If I had worked on the Republican side, I may have become entrenched in the ideology of mistrust for the opposing party. That ideology may be acceptable inside the beltway, where one is a Republican or Democrat first and an American second, but I cannot accept that personally.

The short explanation for my working for a Democrat was that I had no actual choice. Tim Johnson, the junior Senator from South Dakota at the time, was also a Democrat. Therefore, the two Senators from my state who could have appointed me were both Democrats. It made the most practical sense to apply through Daschle because of his position as majority leader. Vermont Senator Jim Jeffords's switch to Independent from Republican had given Daschle and the Democrats a razor-thin majority in the Senate in May 2001. Daschle was in a position to select as many of the pages as he wanted, and he usually took three or four of the thirty or so slots. So the great luck that the majority leader was from my state made it that much easier for me to become a Senate page. Two other pages came from South Dakota, and they became powerful symbols of home for me when we had rough days in the program.

However, the best answer to the question of why I worked for the Democrats came to me after September 11th, because from that day on, we all worked for our great republic and its greatest legislative body—the U.S. Senate. There were no political parties in the first few months after the terrorist attacks because we were all Americans first. I would find that all of the Senators truly loved their country, and it was possible to put partisan differences aside! So I like to follow their lead and explain that I was a U.S. Senate page first, and working on either side of the aisle was secondary.

During orientation at the U.S. Capitol, we met the cloakroom staff who would be acting as my supervisors throughout my service as a page. Three of the four were from South Dakota because Daschle controlled the staffing of this room. Dad enjoyed talking to each of them to learn where in South Dakota each had originally called home. Along with the other pages, I listened intently as the cloakroom staffers explained what we would be doing on a day-to-day basis. I soon realized that most of the training would come on the job. It is pretty hard to explain how to be a page without just stepping into the fire and doing it.

Erik Pederson would be our main supervisor, and he took us on a tour of the cloakroom and Senate floor to help explain the job we were undertaking. Some parents and pages would ask questions along the way, but most were still awestruck by the amazing access we were getting to the U.S. Senate. Erik showed us the telephone booths inside the cloakroom that were reserved for Senators only. He explained that pages would be called on frequently to deliver messages to Senators when they had calls waiting for them in the cloakroom. Pages might even have to interrupt Senators in the telephone booths to deliver new messages to them.

One function of the cloakroom for the pages would be to provide access to water for the Senators. A water cooler stood at one entrance to the cloakroom with a list of all the Democratic Senators next to it. Each Senator had a preference for water. Most noted a request for ice or no ice, and a handful requested club soda instead of water. Erik explained that anytime a Senate leader walked onto the floor, a page should go to the cloakroom for water and put the glass on the Senator's desk. Other Senators would be provided with water if they were coming to the floor to speak or if they requested it directly.

Erik took the group out of the cloakroom and onto the floor. He pointed out some important Senators' desks to the group. Senate leaders Daschle and Trent Lott (R-MS) had desks in the front and center of the chamber with an aisle dividing them. As one looked toward the presiding officer, Daschle sat with his fellow Democrats on the left side of the aisle, and Lott sat on the right side of the aisle. Harry Reid (D-NV) sat next to Daschle, and Don Nickles (R-OK) sat next to Lott. They would serve as assistant leaders for their respective parties and be known as the "whips." Part of their job would be to count votes behind the scenes within their party and "whip" their colleagues onto the party line.

The steps to the rostrum would be our home base. Almost every duty of a Senate page started from these steps. A telephone on these steps could call a page into action in two ways. It could ring in a normal fashion, allowing a page to answer it and receive a verbal command, or it could buzz, which would serve as a nonverbal message to report to the cloakroom. From the cloakroom the page would be sent off on an errand. An individual Senator or staffer could also ask any one of us pages for something while we sat on the steps.

"You'll have to stay alert all the time while on the floor to notice a Senator asking for various items," Erik explained. "Most Senators use specific signals that mean certain things."

Erik demonstrated a drinking motion that would obviously mean that the Senator wanted a drink of water. He then stood behind one of the desks and made a gesture with one hand palm up near the level of the desk and the other hand palm down at about chest level. No one could guess exactly what he might be asking for in this scenario. It looked like he was trying to describe how big something was.

Our answer would be found just off of the Senate floor in the lobby. Erik pointed to another list of Democratic Senators. This time each Senator's name was followed by either "tall," "medium," or "small." These referred to the sizes of the lecterns that each Senator preferred. Now it became obvious that Erik's signal meant that he wanted a lectern on his desk.

"As the majority party, we are responsible for the presiding officer. The pages will monitor the list of Senators that have presiding officer duty for a given day and attend to the needs of each Senator," Erik informed me and the other Democratic pages.

This would be one of the special privileges and responsibilities that the pages for the majority party would have. Democratic senators would take turns in the chair for one-hour shifts. Usually the most junior senators were stuck with the duty, while senior senators only did it if they wanted to. Most senators considered it a mild inconvenience because they would rather be doing other work than performing a largely ceremonial role of presiding over the Senate. Of course, Vice President Dick Cheney, as official president of the Senate, could preside all the time if he wanted to, but he has many other things to do. So junior senators like Hillary Rodham Clinton (D-NY) would be stuck with most of the shifts. We would deliver the gavel to the presiding officer's desk each morning and make sure he or she had a fresh glass of water throughout the day.

All the parents were impressed with the level of day-to-day access that their children would have. Small tasks were being asked of the pages, but these tasks were taking place on such a grand stage that every chore was an honor. Parents began to say goodbye to their children on that Sunday in the late afternoon. For most of the kids involved, it would be their first time away from home for any extended period. For most of the parents involved, it would be the first time that their child's safety would be out of their direct control.

Elizabeth Roach, the Senate Page Program director, and Kathryn Weeden, the Senate Page School principal, assured the families that the pages' safety was the top priority of the program. Strict rules would be in place to protect the teenage pages and the integrity of the program. To their credit, Mrs. Roach and Mrs. Weeden followed through on this promise of safety to the best of their ability despite the unforeseeable events that would follow. To the Senate Page Program's credit, the rules and policies in place helped the other pages and me see each other through the darkest of days and bring more prestige to an historic program.

Senator Daniel Webster appointed the first Senate page in 1829. A nine-year-old boy named Grafton Hanson was the first to have the honor of serving the Senate in this fashion. With the support of Webster and other senators, the service of a single boy soon became a full program staffed by high school-aged males. It would be 1971 before females were allowed to serve as Senate pages. While the Senate program currently allows for approximately 30 pages, the House program calls for nearly 75. Clearly, as the page programs reflected their respective legislative bodies, the Senate side was the more elite upper house!

Our parents were entrusting us to an historic program that obviously valued the work of a young generation. The government saw the value in giving young people an amazing insight into the way Congress works. The

Senate has an interest in keeping their pages safe and giving them the best experience possible. I was told by many different sources that it would be cheaper and more efficient to make the page positions open to college-aged men and women in an unpaid format. The positions would fill up quickly despite the lack of pay. A twenty-year-old worker could accomplish more for the Senate than a sixteen-year-old could even attempt.

But of course, this would tear apart the tradition of a beloved program within the U.S. Senate, a body rooted firmly in tradition. Most Senators would avidly defend the program from such a rationale as cost efficiency. Senator Christopher Dodd (D-CT) had been a page himself. He, like so many other Senators, felt the educational benefits of the program and the adherence to tradition clearly outweighed the government's monetary costs.

Dad had to leave that afternoon after our initial tour of the Senate chamber and cloakroom. We walked outside of Webster Hall toward his rental car with a couple of other pages, whom I would join for dinner at Union Station. But first, the time had finally come for me to say goodbye to my dad. I wanted to stay strong in front of my new friends, so I tried my best to bottle up any emotion. I remember shaking Dad's hand and saying a very mature goodbye while crying like a little kid on the inside. All of us pages were at that amazingly awkward age when we were still children in many ways, yet more mature than most teenagers in other ways.

As I walked alongside some new friends on the three-block journey to Union Station, I processed being on my own for the first time. I didn't realize the irony of my feelings at the time. I would be apart from my family in South Dakota, but I was forming a new familial bond with my fellow pages. I had a Philly steak sandwich at Union Station and talked politics with Patrick Gibson from Illinois, who would quickly be recognized as the most liberal of the pages. So I knew from my first meal "on my own" that I would be experiencing new things and learning a lot from the people around me!

Back at Webster we furthered our orientation process by getting to know our proctors, who would be there for us as disciplinarians and big brothers and sisters. They told us about themselves and explained what they expected from us throughout the semester. Then they forced us to play the cheesiest ice breaker game ever, in which we attempted to learn the names of the other 29 pages. It was definitely one of those things that seems like torture at the time but provides laughs after a couple of weeks, once everyone is comfortable with one another.

We would do some more mandatory bonding on September 3rd when we went to a team-building ropes course. This was the first in a series of field trips that we affectionately called "mandatory fun." We did plenty of different challenges that helped us get to know each other better and build some teamwork and friendship. The task that remains with me today is The Wall. My group of about eight pages and a proctor had to help each other over a wall. The metaphor smacks me in the head like a ton of bricks now, but the whole exercise seemed fairly trite at the time.

The employee of the ropes course explained the rules of the challenge and mentioned the team-building aspect of helping one's teammates get over an obstacle. We pushed each other up and over the wall, with two people staying at the top to help the remaining members. As the second-to-last member to get to the top of the wall, I helped grab our last teammate and pull him over the wall with us. That wall has the honor of being the first obstacle that we climbed over together; there would be many more to come.

We would go to school and work for the first time the next day, September 4, 2001. We would experience a relatively normal routine as pages for just one week before an unimaginably enormous wall would rise in front of us on September 11th.

CHAPTER 3
FIRST WEEK ON THE JOB

I t was the morning of September 4, 2001, and the U.S. Senate was convening after its August recess. Dr. Lloyd Ogilvie delivered the morning prayer in his role as the Senate chaplain. The Senate pages were stationed at all the doors to make sure no one, not even a Senator, interrupted the prayer or the Pledge of Allegiance. Senator Reid led the Senate in reciting the Pledge that morning.

"With liberty and justice for all." And the session had begun.

Now the pages sprang into action for the first time. One Democratic page walked up the rostrum to ceremoniously help the presiding officer into his chair. Four others on the Democratic side headed for the steps of the rostrum. I happened to be the one with the right mixture of stupidity and courage to take the first crack at the "point" position. The "point" page is the page on the rostrum steps furthest from the back wall and closest to the Senators. I was fairly nervous to be first because the page in this position is the most likely to be called upon to run any errands. The Republican side had essentially the same system.

Senator Reid was running the floor that morning, as he would quite often. Another Senator had arrived to replace Reid as presiding officer after the Pledge of Allegiance, so Reid could speak from his normal place on the floor. My first task was obvious enough as Senator Reid began to address the Senate. I had to jump up and go to the cloakroom to get Senator Reid his water. I made it to the cloakroom and checked the list. Reid had the easiest request for his water—no ice. I filled a glass with water, grabbed an official U.S. Senate coaster, and returned to the floor. I set the water on Reid's desk without stepping in front of him, and the day was off to a good start.

We were rapidly absorbing many of the unwritten rules of Senate pleasantries. The first was never to walk in between a speaking Senator and the presiding officer. It is a matter of tradition and respect, as well as a practical issue now that the Senate's deliberations are aired on television. Occasionally, you will see a Senate page on C-SPAN2 walk behind a speaking Senator, or you may see the arms of a page placing water on the desk of a Senator, but you should never see anyone walk across your screen in front of a speaking Senator.

Another rule that we learned quickly in respecting our 100 bosses was that every Senator had the same first name—Senator. "Sir" or "Ma'am" was acceptable, but the term Senator was the best way to address each member. Sometimes we would use the Senator's last name as well to distinguish him or her from the 99 others who apparently shared that same "first name." In a couple of cases, the home state of the Senator would have to be included in order to clarify just which Senator was being discussed. Harry Reid of Nevada and Jack Reed of Rhode Island, both Democrats, had different spellings for their last names, but they sounded the same. Gordon Smith of Oregon and Bob Smith of New Hampshire had a similar problem on the Republican side. The pages and the clerks would refer to these Senators by their states to recognize them correctly.

Recognizing each Senator was a very important part of a Senate page's job. We were given a face book of all 100 Senators early on, and I was tested on identifying the Democratic Senators. I had studied most of the faces before coming to Washington and learned the rest quickly. When handed a note for a certain Senator, it was imperative that a page could recognize that Senator on sight to deliver the message.

The first day of work went by quickly. I noted in my journal some things that seemed incredible to me at the time but would become commonplace as time wore on. That first day, I wrote down the fact that I had

seen Senators Hillary Clinton, John McCain (R-AZ), and Joseph Lieberman (D-CT). To any teenager with a strong interest in politics, these were
three amazing sightings in one day! Clinton was in her first months as
a Senator and a former First Lady. McCain had gained a reputation as
a maverick senator, and I had followed his campaign for the Republican
presidential nomination in 2000. Lieberman had been only a few votes
shy in Florida of becoming president of the U.S. Senate (in other words,
Vice President of the United States). Less than a year earlier, he and Al
Gore had lost their bid for the White House. I would be seeing these three
and many other big names on a daily basis. I must have realized it at the
time, but it obviously hadn't sunk in yet. Every time the Senate voted on
anything from a procedural matter to a judicial nominee, all 100 Senators
would come to the floor in a matter of 15 to 20 minutes. Senators cannot
vote by proxy or phone in their votes; they must come to the floor.

I would never be short of a Senatorial sighting on any given day, but
that is why it's fun to look at my journal from the first week of work to
see how excited I was about the little things before they became commonplace.

Senate pages use the Capitol's elevators frequently to run errands on
the three main levels and the basement. There are elevators reserved for
Senators exclusively, but it is common for a Senator to hop on one of the
other elevators if it is more convenient. On one of my first days on the job,
I rode the elevator with Sen. Jon Kyl (R-AZ). I would ride the elevator
with plenty of other Senators throughout my term as a page, but that first
experience had a simple exhilarating feeling that has stuck with me.

The funniest thing that I wrote down after my first day of work was a
reference to Senator Paul Wellstone (D-MN). After interacting with him
on my first day, I wrote that he was "liberal but incredibly nice," as if being
liberal and nice had been mutually exclusive categories! I would come to
find a deep respect for Senator Wellstone, even though I would disagree
with many of his political stances. We all compared him to our fellow page
Patrick, who was a bleeding-heart liberal himself. We would joke about it

a lot, but we were all learning more and more about people on all parts of the political spectrum.

Senator Mike Enzi of Wyoming stopped by the Democratic side of the rostrum on our first day of work to introduce himself. I was very pleased to see a Senator who personally had no sponsored pages take the time to meet the pages. He was the first Republican Senator with whom I interacted, and he would be the first of many Senators who would be nice enough to take the time to ask how we were doing.

I noted in my journal the next day, September 5th, that another errand I performed was delivering the text of a Senator's speech to the journal clerk for its eventual submission in the Congressional Record. Freshman Senator Maria Cantwell (D-WA) had finished her speech from behind her desk and raised the paper document while making eye contact with me. I walked quickly toward her as she yielded the floor. I took the text from her hand and walked back toward the rostrum to give the document to the journal clerk. He would process it, then give it to another page to deliver down to the basement of the Capitol.

Every word that is said on the Senate floor is marked down by stenographers, but it is much easier to take the actual text of speeches from the Senators directly when possible. The stenographers would come into the chamber on one-hour shifts, much like the presiding officer would. Many of them were very friendly to the pages. They realized that we were new and helped us out in any way they could.

September 5th was also our first day of school. All the pages took four core classes: social studies, science, math, and English. There were different sections of each of these classes. I took American history, physics, pre-calculus, and American literature, in that order, starting at 6:15 AM. With only 30 kids in the whole school, my average class size was about eight students. It was great for individual attention but terrible for trying to sleep!

The early morning classes were a pain, but that wasn't even the beginning. My day would start around 5:15 a.m., when I would get up, shower, and get dressed. We were required to wear suits and ties to class and then on to work. We also had to make sure our rooms were tidy and our beds were made before heading downstairs for breakfast and class. One side of the basement of Webster Hall held a kitchen where we could eat breakfast, and the other area in the basement housed our four classrooms.

Our teachers were top-notch and didn't pull any punches because of the early mornings. In fact, they threw a lot of information at us very quickly because our class time was usually very limited. Even if the Senate was not scheduled to convene until 10 a.m., we would have to be there by 9 a.m., so that left less than three hours for four classes. The Senate would often convene earlier than that, and we would be forced to have severely shortened class periods. It was a challenge that we would become accustomed to.

After an early morning of classes, I walked to the Hart Senate Office Building, went through a set of metal detectors, and headed for the subway system that goes to the Capitol. The tram from the Hart Building to the Dirksen Building and the Capitol was fairly new and ran very well. An older system runs between the Capitol and the Russell Senate Office Building, but I never had any problems with it.

I would begin my duties on the second floor of the Capitol by setting up the Senate chamber for the day's session after checking in with the cloakroom staff. Republican and Democratic pages were responsible for their Senators' desks. Each morning the pages put new documents on each Senator's desk, including the Congressional Record of the previous session. Placed on top of the Record were copies of the most up-to-date Executive and Legislative calendars. The Executive Calendar lists nominations from the President and treaties that are ready for Senate action. The Legislative Calendar is actually titled the Calendar of Business and contains bills and resolutions that are ready for Senate action. These items are placed neatly on the left side of each Senator's desk. The pending bill, resolution, or conference report is placed at the center of the Senators' desks.

Another responsibility that I had the honor of taking on as a page for the majority party was obtaining the gavel for each day's session. The sergeant at arms of the Senate keeps the gavel safely in his office, so two pages would make the trip each morning to take the case with the gavel and a plaque with ceremonial pens for the presiding officer. I would frequently volunteer, both in the morning and at the end of the day's session, to return these items to the sergeant at arms.

Interestingly enough, a new sergeant at arms started his first day of work on September 4, 2001 as well. Al Lenhardt was chosen by the Senate to serve in this function, with responsibility for many matters, including the security of the Senate side of the Capitol. Only a week into his new job, Lenhardt would be challenged with the daunting task of securing a major terrorist target.

When the 100 desks, along with the presiding officer's desk, had been prepared, the Senate was ready to begin its day. We would check the presiding officer list each morning and keep a lookout for the first Senator to have the duty that day. When that Senator and the Senate chaplain gathered near an entrance to the Senate chamber, we knew that they were ready to formally begin that day's session. Half of the pages manned the various doors surrounding the chamber to block off any entrants from disturbing the day's opening ceremonies, which included a prayer and the Pledge of Allegiance.

The Senate would then come to life with Senator Daschle or Senator Reid taking the floor to explain the agenda for the day. Senator Paul Sarbanes (D-MD) was frequently on the floor in the first week of September, as well, because he had been selected to be the manager of the pending legislation, the Export Administration Act. The leadership often designates a Senator to manage the debate on the floor on a specific piece of legislation. The Senator chosen is often a sponsor of the bill, a leader on the committee where the bill originated, or both.

Both the Republican and Democratic pages broke up into two work groups. One group would manage the Senate floor and run all the errands for one hour, and the other group would sit in the lobby doing school work and relaxing. The two groups would rotate the responsibility of staying past 6 p.m. if the Senate remained in session. While I served as a page, I would estimate that the average adjournment was around 7 p.m. It would vary, though, and the "late group" would take a dinner break at 5 p.m. and be responsible for all duties after 6 p.m., whether the Senate adjourned at 6:01 p.m. or 1:00 a.m. The "early group" would work the hour of 5 p.m. to 6 p.m. and then be free to return to Webster Hall.

Each group was led by a "head page." The Democratic pages were led by two great girls, both named Jen. Jen Holden was from Minnesota and selected by Senator Paul Wellstone, and Jen Cohen was from Las Vegas and selected by Senator Kent Conrad. Conrad hails from North Dakota but selected a non-resident of his state because of his personal friendship with Jen's father. The head page stayed on the floor for the full hour and helped organize and direct the tasks of the pages. She would answer the phone on the rostrum when the cloakroom would call, and she would deliver messages on the floor. During a roll call vote, she would keep track of all Democratic Senators who had voted. If a Senator had still not voted late into the scheduled vote, the head page would send another page to go look for that Senator.

At times I wished I was a head page because they got to stay on the floor for the full hour shifts, so they could hear the bulk of a speech by a Senator. My duties required me to leave the floor to run errands in the rest of the Capitol or in the adjacent office buildings, so I would miss some beginnings, middles, and ends of speeches. On the other hand, the head pages would often lament that they didn't get to go exploring the rest of the Capitol like most of the other pages did. On a couple of occasions, we switched roles so everyone got a chance to learn the job of head page in case the head page couldn't make it to work on a given day.

The one-hour break when my group was not on the floor was incredibly valuable for doing school work. It was an amazing feeling to have the lobby of the U.S. Senate turned into a study hall! We worked on homework assigned to us that morning in school with our fellow pages who shared the same classes. In the lobby, it mattered very little if you were a Republican or a Democratic page, because there was no real dividing line. I would often go and sit with Republican pages to study, and they would often come to our side of the lobby.

The setting for our studying made it more exciting to learn. I especially remember the stunning nature of studying my American history text book when I was surrounded by that history in the building where I worked. Senators would often pass through the lobby on their way on or off the floor, and some would ask what we were studying. Senator Barbara Mikulski (D-MD) stopped to talk to a group of us one day as we worked on an American history project, and she emphasized the importance of working together and dividing the labor to get the job done efficiently. When we told Senators that we were studying physics or calculus, they would often joke that they would help if they could, but it was over their heads. It was fun to see some self-deprecating humor and humanizing actions from these Senators that we all looked up to.

Some of us thought that Thursday, September 6th, the scheduled date of a joint session of Congress, would be the biggest event of our term as pages. We were told that a joint session did not occur regularly, with the exception of the President's State of the Union address. We would finish our term as pages just days before President George W. Bush's first such address, so when we learned of the upcoming joint session that we would be able to attend, we were very excited. Mexican President Vincente Fox was visiting Washington, D.C., and would address Congress that day in the House chamber.

Like many other Senate pages, I had never been in the House chamber, so it was an exciting experience for us to walk over to the other side of the Capitol as a group. The speech would not be carried on live network television like the State of the Union, so the publicity around it and the desire of all the members of Congress to attend was lower than usual. Enough Senators and Representatives chose not to attend Fox's speech that there were seats for the Senate pages. It was a great experience to look around the chamber and recognize the Senators and some of the more famous Representatives. Representative Tom Osbourne (R-NE), the former Nebraska football coach, sat in front of me during Fox's speech. One of the other pages sat next to my Republican Representative from South Dakota at the time, John Thune.

President Fox spoke in English for most of the speech and used a translator when he wanted to speak in Spanish. He discussed the new relationship that Mexico and the United States could develop as trust between the two nations grows. Fox noted that Americans may have thought it unwise to trust Mexican governments in the past because of their undemocratic tendencies. Fox assured those present in the House chamber that Mexico was deepening its democratic values and looking forward to working with America on issues like drug trafficking and immigration.

The speech was impressive, but you wouldn't have guessed it if you had been watching some of the Senate pages in the audience. A few days of getting up at 5 a.m. had finally caught up with a couple pages, and they dozed off at various times throughout the speech! The cloakroom staff foresaw this possibility, though, and told us to wake up anyone falling asleep next to us. We tried our best to enjoy the speech and keep everyone awake.

I had my first vocabulary test in English class on that Friday. It was a practical application of the terminology involved in our workplace. Words like convene, adjourn, and filibuster appeared on the quiz. Our teacher, Mrs. Owens, loved to talk about the etymology or origins of words, and I loved to learn about these words with a political nature.

I continued to get settled in Webster Hall on my first full weekend in Washington. The early mornings and long days of work had caught up with me, so I slept in on the weekend. I had made it through my first week as a page! I wondered if the joint session with President Fox would be the highlight of the experience. I had enjoyed my first days as a page, and after catching up on some sleep, I was even more excited to take on the job now that I had a better understanding of what it entailed. I had no way of knowing that my second week in Washington would be the most pivotal, not only of my page experience, but also of my life thus far. There was no way that one week of experience as a Senate page could prepare me for the tests of mind, body, and soul that lay ahead.

Chapter 4
The Wisdom of Senator Byrd

M onday, September 10th, was a vital day for me in the process of coping with the events of September 11th. I would later realize that it was the day that a higher power began to guide me with a loving light through the dark days ahead. A message of hope and love was needed leading into September 11th, and it was delivered.

A simple message of faith would be hammered home to me by one of my 100 bosses, the president pro tempore, no less. Senator Robert Byrd (D-WV) held the position because of his status as the senior member in the majority party. Technically, he was third in succession to the Presidency, only behind Vice President Dick Cheney and House Speaker Dennis Hastert (R-IL). Byrd has represented West Virginia in Congress since 1952 and in the Senate since 1958. Many other Senators told us to seek out Senator Byrd if we had any questions about the history of the Senate because he simply embodied that history.

Byrd did the seeking out on that Monday. He gathered the pages who were in the lobby. He ordered a page to pull out the other pages in the Senate chamber because he wanted to speak to all of us. This would mean that the Senate floor would be void of pages for a while, but no one would question Byrd.

I was standing to his immediate right with all the other pages gathered in a circle around him in the lobby. He asked us how we were all doing and told us that he had a few stories for us. This would be the first in a handful of story sessions with the Senator. It was a great experience for all because he loved to talk, and we loved to listen!

One of his stories that day was a fable about a man who had been told he could have as much land as he could cover by foot in one day. The man would set out in the early morning and would have to turn back and make it to the starting point by sunset. All the land that he could stake for himself would be his. The man walked over the land that morning with excitement in his great opportunity. As he walked, the land grew more and more fertile, so he pressed on to cover as much as he could. The hot sun reached its highest point in the sky, signaling that the day was half over, but the man continued forward, marveling in the rich land that would soon be his.

When he finally decided to turn around, the day was more than half gone. His return journey would be more difficult because he had been given no supplies of food and water, and the sun was beginning to take its toll. His chances for claiming the land were dropping like the sun from the sky. He struggled on until he finally saw the point from which he had started that morning. The sun had nearly set behind him, but he still thought he could make it. He was so tired that he was stumbling desperately toward the "finish line." Fatigue and dehydration finally struck the man as he crawled the last few yards and dropped short of his mark—dead.

Byrd explained the obvious moral of the fable: that the man's greed had not only caused him to get no land, but had ended his life as well. The desire for more and more of the fertile land overrode his better judgment to turn back before the day was half gone. Material possessions can sometimes blind us from the simpler things that make life worth living.

The Senator told us to keep our lives in perspective. He transitioned from discussing the moral of the fable to talking about his belief in a Supreme Being. At age 84 he spoke with hands shaking with some kind of arthritic tick, but his message was smooth and clear. He explained that each of us should be humbled by the fact that we are so small in the grand scheme of things.

"God's plan is so much more than our minds can comprehend," he stated, then turned to me and knocked on my head for a visual aid.

We all chuckled at the simple gesture. When Byrd tapped me on the head, God's important message of hope and love came through. This was a group of some of the brightest and best kids our country had to offer, along with a senior U.S. Senator, but it was obvious that all our knowledge combined could not begin to fathom the plans of the Supreme Being. It wasn't an instant realization or a sudden miracle of any kind, but that moment would become an important milestone in my growing faith.

I would look back to that day's message throughout my time as a Senate page to keep my life in perspective. Byrd did not go on to talk about a set of religious facts of a particular sect, but talked only about the abstract concept of faith. Believing without seeing can be one of the simplest yet most complex challenges of faith. Byrd explained that the first part of this faith is taking a role of humility before God. Another part is recognizing that God's presence is always around us, but not in a material sense. Knowing that God has a plan of infinite wisdom and that He is always present spiritually would be my guiding light through the events of September 11th.

I grew up in a Christian family. I went to Mass with my dad often as a kid. I was baptized and received first communion in the Roman Catholic Church. After my parents divorced, I lived with my mom and began to attend the First United Methodist Church. Now I am a confirmed Methodist with a strong Catholic background and a graduate of a prestigious Catholic university, the University of Notre Dame. Most of my experience has taught me that a lot of the differences between Catholics and Protestants (and among Protestants) are small and involve some level of semantics, but that is not the issue I want to take up here. I am more interested in the big picture of spirituality and God than the minutiae of denominational differences.

The big picture in our great country is that we were founded with a Judeo-Christian philosophy. We have the freedom to exercise our religion as we see fit, and the government cannot establish a certain religion for its people. Despite a secular push for disregarding the importance of religion and spirituality in the public arena, we can still see that the big picture of what our country stands for involves God. The U.S. Senate, for example, begins its day with a prayer asking for a higher power's guidance in its deliberations. The Senate goes on to recite that we are "one nation *under God*" to signify the humility of our government and people. Many powerful Senators take this opportunity to remind themselves that they are not the highest powers in the universe.

It has always been special to me that this message of God's love came to me in Washington, D.C., on September 10th. Some would believe that this is only a coincidence. On the other hand, some believe in a fatalistic type of philosophy where all events that occur were meant to be, regardless of any human action. I don't believe that all the events in my life leading up to and occurring during my Senate page experience can be explained by a simple theory of coincidence. I also don't believe in a fatalism that allows for no control over one's life. I believe that God gives us plenty of chances to make our lives good through our own free will.

While Senator Byrd had great stories and important wisdom to share, I believe it was a message from a much more powerful being than the president pro tempore of the Senate that shone through that Monday.

We would need it on Tuesday.

CHAPTER 5
SEPTEMBER 11, 2001

The U.S. Senate was to convene at 10 a.m. on September 11, 2001. It was a standard time for the Senate to come into session with plenty of appropriations bills and other legislative activity to manage. Before we could begin work, though, we had to make it through a morning of classes.

After a quick breakfast, I strolled into my U.S. history classroom at 6:15 a.m. in full Senate page uniform—a dark navy blue suit with a dark blue tie and my Senate page lapel pin. Mr. Bowers lectured on colonial America and assigned a few pages of reading, along with a worksheet on the Mayflower Compact. I went on to my physics and math classes, and those teachers assigned some homework problems for us out of our textbooks. In American literature we discussed some of the short stories that we had read, and Mrs. Owens assigned more reading for next class time.

I can look back at my school assignment book to this day and see how normal that morning was. For some reason I think I should be able to look at the place in the book for Tuesday the 11th and find something that would suggest the events that would unfold just minutes and hours later. Instead, the assignment book simply documents an average day in the curriculum of a junior in high school.

We got out of that normal day of school with enough time to get to work in the Senate chamber by 9 a.m. I walked to work with a group of other pages, and we cut through the Hart Building as usual to take the underground tram to the Capitol. We rode the elevator up to the second floor from the basement level. The Republican pages among us went into the Republican cloakroom, and the rest of us entered the lobby on our way to the Democratic cloakroom.

We weren't supposed to cut through the Senate chamber with our backpacks still on from school, so we went all the way through the lobby and around to the back entrance of our cloakroom. I put my school bag in the closet along with the others' and made my way to the main desk to sign in for the day of work.

I stopped short of signing in, though, when I saw a couple of cloakroom staffers and some pages who had arrived a few minutes earlier staring at the television in amazement. I looked at the TV for a few moments to try to figure out what was happening. CNN seemed to be covering a story of an accident of some kind in New York. I caught something about a plane hitting a building. I imagined a small private plane losing control in a tragic accident. Just moments after reading the headlines on the screen, I saw a plane come into view and rip through one of the Twin Towers of the World Trade Center with a ball of fire. I thought it must have been a replay of the first plane striking the building, but the news anchors soon explained that this was a different plane altogether.

New York City was the only place affected at this time, and to the best of our knowledge that was the end of it. It all seemed far away at the moment, and the televisions would make it seem far away throughout the day. We had no expectations that the Senate would not still convene at 10 a.m., so we carried on with our duties in setting up the chamber for the day's session.

I remember walking around the Senate floor with a great friend of mine, Kevin Burleson. We were in separate work groups on the Democratic side, but we still managed to do a lot of tasks together. Kevin hailed from Wisconsin and was appointed by Senator Herb Kohl. We were setting up the Senators' desks that morning and running some other errands together. All the while we were speculating about the events in New York and trying to find a rational way that it could all be an accident, but any naïve hopes of this being a tragic accident sunk when we considered that two separate planes had struck the skyscrapers. We realized that two planes hitting the towers could only be explained by an intentional act. I remember that we both held out hope that it would be something less sinister than terrorism, but we had too many tasks to accomplish to go check the news again. I hoped that the Senators themselves would address the issue shortly when we convened.

The U.S. Senate would not get the chance to convene that day, though. All the pages were called to the cloakroom around 9:40 a.m. The cloakroom staff, along with new reports just coming on the television, informed us that the Pentagon had been hit by an airplane.

I didn't know too much about the Washington, D.C., area at the time, but I knew the Pentagon was very close. At the time I would have told you it was in the District itself, but it is actually just outside of D.C. in northern Virginia. Hearing the news from our cloakroom supervisors and then seeing the television switch from images of destruction in New York to coverage of the Pentagon attack was chilling. The news now seemed too close to home for any comfort.

All the Democratic pages sat together as the cloakroom staff explained to us that we might have to evacuate. We all kept calm and began an orderly process of leaving the cloakroom by signing out from work at the main desk. The idea of simple paperwork got ditched quickly in the next moments with the entrance of a Capitol Police officer. He addressed our cloakroom supervisors, stating firmly that we all needed to evacuate "right away."

We all understood the urgency of his words. Other than a quick stop at the closet to grab our school bags, we evacuated without delay or hesitation. I gathered outside with about seven other pages. Both of my fellow South Dakotans were in this group. Katie Ruedebusch lived six hours west of me on the other side of the state in Rapid City. Jason Frerichs of the small town of Wilmot was the only true farm kid of my page class, and he made Katie and me feel like real city-slickers.

As we headed toward the Russell Building and away from the Capitol, Jason and I tried to keep everyone together. I'll admit that I felt a little lost. I probably could have made it back to Webster Hall on my own, but I was glad I didn't have to try. It was the first time that we had left the Capitol by other means than the underground tram system.

Other eerie circumstances made the otherwise simple walk more difficult. I saw many people on the streets trying to use their cell phones. Many of them had evacuated their own buildings or had already been outside when all the evacuations began. Regardless, they were all trying to get more information on the situation or let others know what was happening. Many of the people did a double-take as our group walked quickly past them. I imagine that a group of half-lost-looking 16-year-olds running out of the Capitol troubled many of these adults on various levels.

Jason and I continued moving forward, and he soon confirmed that he knew where he was going. That was the good news. As we walked further from the Capitol, we were moving away from the bad news, which was the Pentagon. Before trees and other government buildings blocked the line of sight, I could see the smoke coming up from the Pentagon. That had been my first real image of the September 11th attacks. The television could never show me a picture or tell me a story as powerfully as I could see it for myself.

I knew that Jason had the group's course under control, so I looked back at Katie and the others. Two of the girls back with Katie were sobbing loudly. The emotion of the past moments had hit them before it would hit me. The reality of the situation was apparent, but the adrenaline and instinct in my system had not given way to any emotions yet. I looked back again as we neared Webster Hall and saw the other half of the group of Democratic pages following us. All the Republican pages had evacuated just after we did and were following behind.

We were the first eight pages back to Webster. The staff there was waiting for us and directed us downstairs to the classrooms. I went into my English classroom to use the phone to call home. As I dialed the numbers, I tried to think of what I was going to say. I didn't know if my mom had seen the reports on TV, so I thought that I might have to explain the entire situation. When I stopped to think about the situation as a whole, the emotions of the ordeal began to come to the surface. I struggled to speak smoothly with a frog in my throat, and I blinked hard to hold back any tears. Thankfully, my mom had been watching the news, so I didn't have to explain much. I kept the conversation short so that the emotion wouldn't overcome me and the other kids could use the phone after me.

Seeing the smoke rise from the Pentagon fell to second on my list of big reality checks after I talked to my mom. My mom did a great job of reassuring me by simply saying that she understood the situation and would talk to me later. The straightforward words and sentences that we spoke did not lend themselves to too much emotion. The calm and even tone that she used reassured me that I was safe at that moment. It was the initial recognition of the voice as that of my mother that struck the right chord. In a time of such trouble, hearing the voice of a person concerned with nothing but my well-being made the gravity of the situation sink in a bit deeper.

That conversation with anyone else in the world would not have had the same effect on me. Hearing my mother's voice would set the tone for my thought process for the rest of the day. After that phone call, I would have plenty of time to watch the events unfold and reflect on what exactly these attacks could mean for the future.

I moved to another classroom where some others had gathered to watch the television. I didn't grasp the irony at the time, but I was watching an event of massive historical importance unfold in my American history classroom. After a few minutes of watching the news, we had the basic facts of the situation confirmed. The planes that had hit the towers in New York, along with the plane that hit the Pentagon, had been hijacked and purposely flown into the buildings. At some point that morning, the reports came in that a fourth plane had crashed in Pennsylvania, but there was only speculation on what exactly had occurred aboard that aircraft.

I don't remember connecting the dots that morning to realize that the fourth plane could have had the Capitol as its target, but I do remember feeling thankful in general that the Capitol was not hit. As I watched the horrific scenes play out in New York and at the Pentagon, I could not help but feel a connection to the sites that were attacked. All of us would come to realize at one time or another that we worked in a building that symbolized democracy; therefore, we worked in a building with a constant bull's-eye on it.

I looked around the small classroom to get a sense of how everyone else was doing. Most sat stunned on the desks or in the chairs with their eyes either fixated on the television screen or purposely avoiding the images. Nearly all the eyes held some water, standing ready to trickle down in the form of tears at any moment. Everyone had reached a family member, so we had nothing to do but sit and wait.

I specifically remember one of my roommates, Jay Wright, calling his parents in the history classroom while sitting at Mr. Bowers's desk. I didn't listen in on any of the conversation, but I could see the same emotions play out in the same manner as they had during my phone call minutes earlier. Jay's eyes began to water as he listened to his father's voice on the other end, and he blinked back the tears.

I made eye contact with him moments after his conversation home and simply nodded my head to him. He nodded back with the same simple recognition of understanding. We were all in the same boat. All of us were juniors in high school and had said goodbye to our parents just over a week ago. We had to have known that we would miss our families, but it was impossible to have known how much we would need them. We didn't necessarily need them right there holding our hands and wiping our tears. We were big kids, but we were still kids. Each of us needed that phone call. We needed to hear that voice of a loved one.

After we had made our phone calls, we all had the comfort of knowing that our families were aware of our safe evacuation from the Capitol. As we sat around in the classrooms in the basement of Webster, I realized that each person was in his or her own little world. Some might have been trying to sort out the information on the television or deal with their own fear. All must have continued to think of their families, especially the comfort that comes from parents. I looked around the room and made eye contact with some other pages. It wasn't a full realization at that moment, but it began to click that even though none of our parents could be there for us directly, we could all be there for each other.

The events of this day affected us in such a way that we bonded faster and grew closer together than most classes of Senate pages. We moved from simple coworkers to close friends naturally, and we moved from close friends to family out of necessity. It didn't happen instantaneously, but we all knew that we couldn't handle the enormity of the situation alone. We needed family, so we became family.

The enormity of the situation was better realized when the Twin Towers fell to the ground in New York. First, a few floors from the top of one of the buildings crumbled away. I remember thinking that anyone who was still alive and in those top floors of the building was now gone. My heart sank at the stark finality of it, but I thought that at least the people below the entry points of the planes could still get out of the building. This high hope for the rescue and survival of any others in the building came crashing down with the tower as it seemed to implode on itself.

"Oh my God!" was the quiet exclamation from a few, but most were deadly silent in the classroom where I sat. The other classroom with a television must have experienced the same stunned response because I did not hear anything from down the hall. It was a bit too much to bear the realization that many people must have lost their lives in that instant when the tower came down like a wave.

Another assessment of the room would find some with tears streaming down their faces and others with their heads down in sorrow. All was quiet and still, though. No one really sobbed or made a sound of any kind for a few minutes.

"Will the other tower face the same fate?" I thought to myself. It had to have been the thought on everyone's mind. Any optimism was now cautious optimism. The second tower would hold on only a half-hour longer, and the same shock would overtake us. Even though we had seen the first tower come down, the second tower's collapse was just as powerful, if not more so. After the second tower was gone, there was nothing. That absence of any structure at all was more frightening than a burning building. We all know that firemen can rescue people in a burning building, but what happens when there's no building left at all?

Compounding the terrible developments in New York were reports on the damage at the Pentagon. Even more, some false reports came in of other attacks near our position in the nation's Capitol. I heard a report of a car bomb exploding outside of the Supreme Court. I wondered if we would have been close enough to hear an explosion if this had been true. Other reports and rampant speculation made us wonder if the attack was just beginning.

Hindsight allows us to limit the attacks to the four planes, but while we were in the moment, there was no way of knowing just when the strikes had ended. With this mindset it made sense for us to evacuate further. The program staff worked out the logistics to get all of the pages out of D.C. and into a hotel in Maryland.

The program staff told us to go upstairs and start boarding the vans outside of the dormitory. Now that we had something to do besides watch the television, we made our way out of our state of shock. We were not allowed time to pack an overnight bag or bring anything from our rooms. We boarded the vans and waited until everything was in place to evacuate.

I didn't know where exactly we planned on going or how long it would take to get there. The element of shock gave way to a new sense of fear of the unknown. When we had evacuated the Capitol, there had been fear because we hadn't known exactly what was going on, and we had had to journey back to Webster Hall by a new route. As we evacuated D.C., we knew the nature of the attacks, but we didn't know if they were finished.

On the drive we would learn that we were headed to Maryland for the night. The traffic was fairly heavy leaving the city (granting that any traffic seems heavy to a South Dakotan!). I watched the activity on the roads and looked for signs to figure out exactly where we were going.

Sometimes the best parts of school field trips and sporting events on the road were the actual drives themselves. Traveling with my high school tennis team had always been fun because we would tell jokes and play cards. I remember basketball trips being loud and rambunctious throughout middle school. This trip from D.C. to Maryland was not one of those occasions. All the passengers were fairly subdued. No one had experienced anything like this, so no one knew exactly what to say.

We monitored the radio reports as we rode. Very little new information was provided, but we listened closely nonetheless. It was a good feeling to be moving further away from all the potential targets in Washington. The only other feeling that started to come upon us was hunger.

Our caravan of Senate pages pulled into Chesapeake Beach, Maryland, as the lunch hour approached. We stopped at a seafood restaurant. I'm not sure if the staff had called ahead or not, but the restaurant made room for about thirty Senate pages and a handful of support staff. Driving the government vans, our four proctors had evacuated with us, as had the program director.

I sat down at a table with Jay and a couple of other pages. We ordered our food and tried to make light conversation as best we could. We were away from news broadcasts of any kind for the first time since we had evacuated the Capitol by foot. It was a blessing to be away from the reporters' speculation and the horrific images for a while. Some of our own speculation would find its way into our conversations, though, as little else was on our minds.

The restaurant was located right on the sea front, so some of us made our way outside to the docks after the meal. We milled around in small groups for a while. Someone pointed out some jellyfish in the water and some nice boats tied to the docks, and we gathered around to see. Normally, a scene like this would spark some great conversations about boating or fishing, but no one felt very talkative yet. Many of the small groups broke down even further as people decided to find a spot to themselves along the beachfront and others gathered in a picnic area.

"We were literally shell-shocked," I would write in my journal regarding the time meandering outside of this restaurant.

The program staff gave us plenty of time to get our bearings and begin to sort through the events of the morning. They took the time to further plan and coordinate our evacuation. They made arrangements for us to spend at least one night in a nearby Holiday Inn Express.

I went out close to the water and sat on the rocks. It was the first time that I was by myself on that day with no television distractions or worries about further evacuation. It was the first time that I could reflect clearly on the events of the morning and begin to gain perspective. I found it important to think about all those who were injured and killed earlier that day. I looked out over the water and tried to put my situation into perspective.

First, I thought back to the horror of the attacks caught on camera in New York. Those events on television seemed far away, but then I remembered the smoke that I had seen first-hand rising from the Pentagon. I thought of all the people who had been in the World Trade Center and in the Pentagon. I remember groaning inside at the thought of people trying to escape the towers but not making it out before the collapse.

I thought about all the people in the hijacked airplanes and how their lives had been cut short in an instant as terrorists used the planes as weapons. At the time I didn't know much about Flight 93, the plane that had crashed in Pennsylvania, but I grieved knowing that there could be no survivors from that crash.

I thought of all these lives being taken away on one ordinary morning. That's when the first pang of guilt hit me. All those people were gone, and I was still here. I was in a building that was just as important a target as any in the country, but I was spared. I was hard on myself for a few minutes. I scolded myself for taking life for granted, to whatever degree.

"For what reasons did I come here?" I asked myself. I realized that some of those reasons were selfish. I had come to D.C. with hopes that the experience would help me make connections with important people and boost my résumé. While the idea of service to my country and the U.S.

Senate had been part of my original motivation, it seemed more important now than ever. I vowed to improve my priorities with a new perspective after that morning, a morning when the value of life itself was highest.

I remember looking out over the water and thinking how beautiful a day it was. There were a small number of white, fluffy clouds up against a pure blue sky. The sun shone brightly and reflected off the smooth surface of the water. I look back on the beauty of nature that day and see God's presence. Metaphorically, people will always refer to September 11th, 2001, as a terribly dark day, but God shone through with the beautiful light of nature in order to let us know that He was still watching over us.

I sat on those rocks for at least twenty minutes before another page approached me. By the end of the program, I knew Scott Moore as a dear friend and brilliantly witty character. At this point I knew him only as the page from Kentucky, and it wasn't the right time for him to display his humorous wit, so he simply asked if I was OK.

"Yeah, Scott. Thanks. Just taking a few minutes to gather some thoughts, you know?" I responded as I stood up from the rocks.

Scott gave a nod of understanding and carried on past me. I looked to see where he was headed, and I saw many of the pages gathering near our vehicles again. I took a couple more moments to look across the water and out to the horizon where the water met the sky, and then turned to join the others.

We loaded up the vehicles and headed for the hotel. I arrived at the Holiday Inn Express with a sense of relief in knowing that we would be out of harm's way with a safe place to spend the night. We had none of the amenities that one would normally take along when staying away from home. We had no toothbrushes, toothpaste, contact solution, deodorant, or even changes of clothes. Our proctors dealt with the situation as best they could. They got us some of the essentials at the hotel's front desk and made arrangements for us to go to Wal-Mart that evening to pick up some other items.

In the meantime we could only watch television in our hotel rooms and begin to speculate on who these terrorists could be. Each set of roommates got one hotel room. My three roommates and I took turns calling our parents again. There wasn't much news to tell them, other than that we were safe in a hotel in Maryland. They relayed some information to us, but we were already catching up on the news ourselves quickly enough.

There was a report on TV about a possible declaration of war. It was proposed in a unique way because it was unlikely that another sovereign state had attacked us, but rather a rogue terrorist group. As Osama bin Laden became the key suspect in the attacks, some analysts debated the possibility of making an official declaration of war against him personally. It was an amazing line of thinking that I could never have imagined before that morning. Any kind of declaration of war would have to go through the Congress, so we talked with excitement about the possibility of the U.S. Senate taking up the debate on how to respond to these attacks. That afternoon we did not have any clear sign that the Capitol would be reopening for business the next day, though.

The first time I remember smiling and having a decent laugh that day was on our trip to Wal-Mart. We were all stressed to the max, and we laughed at ourselves and at our awkward situation of having no personal belongings with us. I went in on some contact solution and a package of underwear with another page, and I bought some comfortable sweatpants to lounge in for the rest of the evening. The only shoes I had were my dress shoes, so I looked for some slippers. I bought a pair of brown, corduroy slippers that were about two sizes too big. They were ridiculous! One of the other pages dubbed them "grandpa slippers," and we all had a good laugh. Soon, a couple of our proctors would be calling me "Grandpa Joe" because of the slippers, and the nickname stuck pretty well.

Some fun continued back at the hotel as we played some games in one of the conference rooms. This laid-back activity was great because it took our minds off the events of the day, and we got to begin the process of growing closer together as a group. It was important for us to be able to look back at that day and have some light-hearted memories.

My roommates and I had our TV on as we got ready for bed that evening. We listened for any new developments, and we wondered if the Congress would be going back to work in the Capitol the next day. Our answer came with a knock on the door and entrance of Mr. Joseph Hampel, the only male proctor. He told us that the Senate would be convening the next morning.

With his next sentences he spoke slowly and carefully. He explained that the Senate would be asking for some pages to volunteer to come back to work the next morning. He emphasized that we did not have to go back and that the Senate would be able to get along with a very limited number of pages if necessary.

The four of us looked at each other for a moment to gauge one another's enthusiasm for jumping back into the thick of things. I remember having a serious hesitation in my mind about going back to work on September 12th, but at the same time I could sense that it would be an important thing to do. Jay spoke up firmly to say that he would volunteer. I followed suit immediately, as did my two other roommates.

We were the last room down the hallway that Mr. Hampel visited that evening. He thanked us for volunteering in a way that made me think that maybe no one else had volunteered. This made me second-guess myself for a couple of reasons. First, maybe we were simply crazy to go back into the Capitol Building the day after an attack that might not be fully over. Second, I knew that the Senate could not be run by only four pages. We would be stretched thin on a busy day with all thirty pages.

One of my roommates must have had the same thoughts going through his head, because he asked Mr. Hampel if any others had volunteered. He informed us that all of the guys had volunteered, and most of the girls, as well. My earlier doubts evaporated when I realized we would be going back to Washington with nearly our full force. It confirmed to me that it was the right thing to do. Even the three girls who had decided not to go to work still went back into D.C. and to Webster Hall. We were all back to work by September 14th, so it was clear that we would not let the terrorists set our agenda.

I must commend Majority Leader Daschle and Speaker Hastert for truly standing up to the enemies of freedom by making the decision to bring the Congress back the next morning. Before a single Senator spoke that morning, the winning message of democracy was already ringing back to Osama bin Laden. Getting back to work with the people's business was essential to begin the healing.

President Bush summed up the necessary resolve when he said, in a televised address to the nation on the evening of September 11th, "Terrorist attacks can shake the foundations of our biggest buildings, but they cannot touch the foundation of America." Hearing those words from the President and witnessing the decisions of the leadership in Congress, there was no shortage of inspiration that day.

There would be no official declaration of war on Osama bin Laden or his evil network, but we would soon be fighting in a conflict like none other in our history. It was obvious that my generation would be the one that needed to respond. My grandparents were part of the Greatest Generation, with one of my grandfathers fighting in WWII and the other in the service during the Korean War. They preserved our freedoms at a heavy price with the Cold War on the horizon.

My parents' generation saw the decline of the Soviet Union and sent me off to elementary school as the Berlin wall collapsed. After September 11th a new war was laid on the doorstep of my generation. Would we stand up willingly to make the necessary sacrifices? Would we rise to the challenge with the necessary courage? Would we maintain integrity through the strength of character? Would we fight evil by doing good for others?

Leaders like Tom Daschle and George W. Bush could inspire my generation, but they could not answer these questions on their own. My generation would have to speak for itself—and speak we did. The next day, footage of the U.S. Senate would be played throughout the world, and young kids could be seen stepping up to the plate in service. The U.S. Senate pages were back at work with a front row seat to the amazing events of the days that would follow the cowardly acts of terrorists.

In the armed forces, young men and women just a couple of years older than my fellow pages and I were mobilized to Afghanistan just weeks after the initial attacks. These soldiers, marines, sailors, and airmen would bring the fight to the terrorists and liberate a nation of people. Two and a half years after September 11th, President Bush called on troops my age and even a year or two younger to take the objectives of the War on Terror to Iraq. These young men and women embodied the courage and character that our nation needed to preserve its freedoms. And my generation has seen its own casualties and made many sacrifices.

While our armed forces began the military action of this new war in October 2001 in the far away land of Afghanistan, my generation had already begun to make its stand for liberty. We responded less than 24 hours after the attack by returning to Washington, D.C., and serving the U.S. Senate. We started the fight against an incredible evil through service to our country's democracy and all that it represented.

Let it be known throughout the world that our generation responded quickly and decisively with the decision to go back to work on September 12, 2001.

CHAPTER 6
THE RETURN TO WORK

As I walked out to the lobby of the hotel the next morning to gather with the rest of the group to head back to Washington, I picked up a *USA Today* with the headline "Act of War." It hadn't been just a bad dream after all. The main picture on the front page of the newspaper was of the explosion from the second plane striking the World Trade Center.

I looked around at my fellow pages. We all looked a little wearied and tired, but that wasn't unexpected. We had been running on little sleep for the past week, and we were wearing essentially the same set of clothes as yesterday.

I had no idea what the day of work would entail. I had learned in my first week of work that every day would be different, and it is difficult to describe an "average" day on the Senate floor. If there ever was an average day in the Senate, I knew this day would not be it. I hopped into one of the vans to head back to Washington, reassuring myself that things would be made safe.

I remember sitting next to Jen Holden in the van on the way back to D.C. that morning. She was the head page for the other Democratic page work group. Jen would get to sit on the rostrum steps for one-hour shifts throughout the day and listen to some of the most powerful people in the world speak on the terrorist attacks. I would work in the Senate chamber on the opposite hour shifts from Jen's and listen to the speeches in between running errands around the Capitol complex. In hindsight, it was clearly an exciting day to be a Senate page, but that morning I could sense a nervous excitement in Jen and all the others that came with the fear of the unknown.

When we arrived at the Capitol, a heightened security presence ushered us into our place of work. The only other thing that was different from past days at work was the presiding officer's desk. It had already been set up on the morning of September 11th, and in the rush to evacuate the Capitol, it had not been a priority to return the gavel to its nightly resting place. Instead, the gavel sat waiting to be slammed by a Senator to signal the official return to the people's business. That Senator would be President Pro Tempore Robert Byrd, and it seemed appropriate because he proved to be the Senator who often produced the most emphatic raps of the gavel.

I was not surprised to see Byrd take the role of presiding officer that morning. He would most likely tell you that it was his honor and privilege to do so. Only Vice President Cheney could have pulled rank on Byrd, but Cheney was certainly hidden in an "undisclosed location" for security reasons that day.

I was slightly surprised to see the full chamber that Byrd was preparing to preside over. I would estimate that the average number of Senators on the floor at a given time (excluding roll call votes) would be three or four, including the Senator serving as presiding officer. Senators simply have places to be and constituents to serve elsewhere if they are not presiding over the Senate, managing the current legislation, or formally addressing the body.

Except for some previous roll call votes, for which all 100 Senators had come through the chamber in a matter of 15 to 20 minutes, the Senate chamber was as crowded as I had ever seen it that morning for the opening prayer and Pledge of Allegiance. Many Senators stood behind their desks, many staffers stood along the back wall, all the usual government officials like the parliamentarian took their places, and all the Senate pages lined the perimeter of the chamber, guarding the doors. All those present prepared to bow their heads to join in a solemn prayer and then place their right hands over their hearts to join in honoring our flag.

"RAP! RAP!" sounded the gavel.

"The Senate will come to order. Our prayer will be delivered by the Senate chaplain, Dr. Lloyd John Ogilvie," Byrd proclaimed.

The chaplain delivered the morning's prayer in a deep, melancholy voice. He prayed for all those who had lost their lives and asked for guidance on how to move forward. "Remind us of how You have been with us in trouble and tragedies of the past and have given us victory over tyranny. Bless the women and men of this Senate today as they join with President Bush in decisive action," he prayed.

Byrd led the Pledge, and despite the many others reciting along with him, I could discern his voice the whole way. Most Senators would lead off the Pledge loudly, then fade back and blend in with the chorus, but Byrd always spoke emphatically. Everyone always stayed with Byrd on the recitation even if he hung on a word or phrase longer than normal. He was the 84-year-old leader, and we were all the followers when it came to the Pledge.

The Senate sprang to life as Byrd took his seat overlooking the chamber. I soon found out that the assigned shifts and work groups meant nothing today. Everyone wanted to be on the rostrum listening to speeches as much as they could. Most of the pages only took a few breaks in the lobby, and those breaks only came when the rostrum steps were too full to squeeze in another body. It would turn into a busy day quickly with plenty of errands to run for the Senators, and each of us listened intently as the Senate leadership addressed the issues of the day first.

Because of the various tasks and errands that were asked of me as a Senate page, I could not listen to all of the Senators' speeches in their entirety. I do remember certain Senators' comments that struck a chord with me, and I've since consulted the Congressional Record for this day to fill in the gaps. Almost all 100 Senators would come to the floor on that Wednesday and into Thursday to speak on the resolution condemning the terrorist attacks. Each Senator had a unique perspective and gave a powerful speech, but I can't reference each Senator here. I will, however, provide some quotes and commentary on some of the most meaningful subject matter of the day.

Senator Daschle, as the majority leader, was recognized first. He took the opportunity to thank the chaplain for his prayer and to thank the Republican leader, Trent Lott, for the bipartisan cooperation with regard to decision-making throughout September 11th. He went on to explain the schedule for the debate on the resolution. Ten minutes would be given to every Senator who wished to speak, with priority given to the leadership and to the Senators from New York and Virginia, because their states had been the sites of the attacks.

Daschle took a few minutes for his personal comments on the events of the previous day. He referred to the decision that was made with other leaders in the Senate and the leadership of the House of Representatives to come back into session.

"Last night we sent the message to the world that even in the face of such cowardly and heinous acts, the doors of democracy will not close. This joint resolution we laid down today condemns yesterday's attacks, expresses our sympathy for the victims and our support for the President as our commander in chief," Daschle said in his passionate yet mild-mannered style.

The Republican leader was the next to be recognized, and after he thanked his Democratic counterpart personally, he commented on the steps to move our nation forward.

"There's much to do. We've got to find out how this happened. Congress has a right and a responsibility to learn what has happened here. We must find out who did it. And we must be prepared to take actions and fight terrorist attacks in the future," Lott said from behind his desk directly across the aisle from Daschle.

Harry Reid, the assistant majority leader or majority whip, was next in line to address the Senate. By this time many of the Senators who came to participate in the opening prayer and to hear the schedule from Daschle had left the floor. However, there were still quite a few Senators milling about and trying to make deals with other Senators about the order of speaking following the New Yorkers and Virginians.

Senator Reid frequently ran through the formalities of parliamentary procedure on the floor to get simple business accomplished. He was usually the first Senator recognized on a given day and the Senator to call for adjournment at 7:00, 8:00, or later in the evening. One could call him the hardest worker on the floor itself, as he was frequently the first to arrive and the last to leave.

The Senator from Nevada brought an interesting perspective on the Wednesday morning after the Capitol had been evacuated. He is a former Capitol Police officer.

"I personally express my appreciation to our Capitol Police men and women who yesterday acted so brilliantly, so heroically, in being called to arms, literally, at a moment's notice. I am very proud of the Capitol Police. We all should be. Every day they put their lives on the line for us," Reid stated.

In the next few days, I would get the chance to interact with some Capitol Police officers personally. I learned that they were working many extra hours to ensure that the Capitol complex was as safe as it could be. The officers often assured me that we were in the safest place in all of Washington. It was strange to think that the biggest target for terrorists in our nation's capital was also the safest place to be. I grew to trust the Capitol Police more and more as other security issues arose, and they solved them. I was happy to hear Senator Reid praise these men and women because he was the most qualified to give that praise.

As I learned more about the heroic stories of the New York firefighters and police, I realized that the Capitol Police would have done the same things had the Capitol been hit. These people would have rushed in to save other people. People like Daschle and Lott could decide to bring the Senate into session in the wake of terrorist attacks, but it was the Capitol Police who made it possible to accomplish that work safely. They deserve a great amount of credit, right along with their counterparts who protect New York City.

Many personal stories would come out of New York City. We would get a chance to hear some of them on the floor of the Senate that morning. Democrat Chuck Schumer of New York was the first Senator to speak after the leadership. Some familiar with politics might express amusement that Schumer was right there with a speech ready to go for the C-SPAN2 audience. The joke in Washington is that the most dangerous place to be is in between Schumer and a television camera! On many issues where partisan politics are apparent, I would say that the joke has a bit of truth to it, but there were no political parties on this day. Schumer spoke from the heart with the pain that many of his constituents were feeling at that very moment.

"I know someone on the 104th floor who worked for the good firm of Cantor Fitzgerald. We can't find hardly anybody from that firm. He called his parents, told them he loved them, and they haven't heard from him since," Schumer shared with the Senate.

The focus then shifted to a Senator representing Virginia, the state where the Pentagon sits. Republican Senator John Warner was the ranking member on the Armed Services Committee at the time and spoke of his contact with President Bush and Defense Secretary Donald Rumsfeld on September 11th. He informed the other Senators that he and Armed Services Committee Chairman Carl Levin (D-MI) had toured the destruction at the Pentagon at the request of Rumsfeld.

"We will never be the same as a nation. That is true. We will be a better nation. We will be a stronger nation, as we step up to meet this challenge...Just a personal note, I remember World War II. I was a youngster in the early parts of it. My generation, at age 17, we all volunteered, in the fall of 1944, 1945. I became a sailor," Warner said, expressing the generational nature of this new challenge. He went on to say that the younger generation would pick up this task and go beyond what the "greatest generation" achieved in WWII to become an even greater generation and to create an even greater country.

The junior Senator from New York would now have her turn to speak. She was still relatively new to the U.S. Senate, but the American people recognized her and her name better than most from her time as First Lady. Hillary Clinton brought this perspective to the floor to show her support to a growing spirit of unity.

"I have expressed my strong support for the President, not only as Senator from New York but as someone who for eight years had some sense of the burdens and responsibilities that fall on the shoulders of the human being we make our President. It is an awesome and at oftentimes awful responsibility for any person. I know we are up to it, I know we are ready for it, and I know that everyone in this body represents every American in making clear that we are united and stronger than ever," Clinton said from her desk in the back of the chamber.

She was a "backbencher" in the literal sense. Her junior status in the Senate itself gave her a low ranking in the seating assignments, but her elevated status and recognition with the American public at large gave her words a high priority.

The flow of the Senatorial speeches was rolling now. I remember being on the floor at one point when the presiding officer was asked what the speaking schedule amounted to at the time. That presiding officer listed off five or six Senators who had already claimed a spot, which meant that there was about an hour-long waiting list to address the chamber.

Before any other Senator could speak, Republican Senator George Allen of Virginia would close out the speeches of the four Senators hit the hardest on September 11th. Allen began explaining a resolution that he and Senator Barbara Boxer (D-CA) had planned to bring to the Senate's attention that week that would condemn suicide bombings in the Middle East.

"We now see with great shock and horror, that the United States is obviously not impervious to these suicide bombings and such attacks," Allen stated the unavoidable truth.

Allen also extended the praise for the heroes in New York and added, "The same was happening in Virginia where we have lost many lives, untold numbers, as of yet, at the Pentagon as well as the passengers on Flight 77 flying from Dulles, VA, that was hijacked and crashed into the Pentagon."

The terrorist attacks not only affected New York and Virginia directly, but the rest of the country and the international community as well. Senator Joe Biden (D-DE) chaired the Foreign Relations Committee at the time of the attacks. He took to the floor early that morning to emphasize the need to unite as a nation and as an international community to condemn terrorism.

"This is not a struggle over ideology. This is not a struggle over religion. This is a struggle between civilization and barbarity," Biden explained. "Let there be no doubt that the United States and civilized nations of the world will unite and win this struggle."

Biden managed much of the speaking order on the Democratic side that morning, which symbolized to me that the issue of the September 11th attacks was taking on an international scope quickly. Biden's Foreign Relations Committee and Levin's Armed Services Committee would become key groups of decision makers in beginning the War on Terror.

My fellow Senate pages and I would often speculate on which Senators would run for the White House. President Bush would obviously be the nominee for the Republicans, but the Democratic field was wide open. It has been said that the Senate is filled with 100 people that want to be President, but John F. Kennedy was the last to be directly elected to the White House as a sitting U.S. Senator. We threw around the name of John Edwards (D-NC) but thought he might be too inexperienced as a freshman Senator. Hillary Clinton was mentioned but deferred in our minds to the 2008 race. John Kerry (D-MA) was the person who seemed the most probable to be the nominee from the pool of candidates in the Senate.

It is interesting to look back on Senator Kerry's words from September 12, 2001, in the context of his presidential bid in 2004.

"What happened yesterday was terrible and horrendous, but we must prepare ourselves and steel ourselves for the possibility of worse until we achieve our goal. And to do that we have to be more prepared than we are today, and we have to take the fight wherever we need to, and in ways that we are, frankly, not yet prepared," Kerry lectured and then cited his own experiences in Vietnam.

The negative campaign against Kerry, who, as a presidential candidate, raised questions about the war in Iraq, would label him as a "flip-flopper" and question the validity of his status as a war hero, and he did take a tumble because of it. I've heard some analysts say that the best speech of Kerry's campaign was his concession speech, which, of course, came after the election was over and bashing Bush was no longer the priority. I would add to that idea that Kerry gave one of the better statements on September 12, 2001, because bashing Bush was the furthest thing from anyone's mind.

As a fellow American, he informed the public that there might be even harder days ahead. As a U.S. Senator, he supported taking "the fight wherever we need to" and voted to go into Afghanistan and Iraq. As a veteran of the guerilla war in Vietnam, he explained that we needed to become more prepared for this new kind of war. It simply turned out that he was a better American, U.S. Senator, and U.S. Navy veteran than he was a presidential candidate opposite George W. Bush.

Another big name that we pages loved to talk about was Senator John McCain. He would often storm on or off the Senate floor either in a hurry or appearing mad about something. The Senate pages near the doors knew to get out of his way or hold the door for him as he passed through. We knew his amazing history as a prisoner of war, and we all admired him for his dedicated service to the armed forces and in the Senate. Once in October as the nation began to commit troops to the fighting in Afghanistan, I remember McCain storming off the Senate floor and past a group of other pages and me. I joked with the others that we could win the war in Afghanistan a lot quicker by just sending McCain over there as our best weapon! We all laughed but also rallied around the idea of McCain's power having a great effect in the War on Terror.

On September 12th, McCain got his chance to speak in the afternoon. His best line was not delivered at the beginning or closing of his speech, but right in the middle. I was organizing some papers just off the floor in the lobby, and each time the nearest door was opened, I could hear the Senator speaking in a firm and polite voice. Once, when the door was held open for a longer period of time, I heard the most powerful statement of the day.

"I say to our enemies, we are coming. God may show you mercy. We will not," McCain stated with such firmness that I not only believed his words, but knew that he was the right person to speak them.

The resolution condemning the terrorist attacks came to a vote before all Senators had spoken on the issue. The leadership pushed the vote to take place so that the Senators from New York and others could return to their home states for important work. All Senators would still get a chance to speak regarding the resolution, but the time allowed would eventually be cut to five minutes because of the enormous turnout by the Senators.

A roll call vote is an amazing sight to see. The clerk reads through all 100 names alphabetically, looking up after each name to see if that Senator is present to vote yet. After going through the list once, the clerk will announce the Senators voting in the affirmative and in the negative. The Senators who have not yet voted will then be allowed to make their vote known to the clerk on a first-come, first-served basis. This whole process takes approximately 15 to 20 minutes. It is much more exciting than a voice vote, for which the Senators vote by saying "aye" or "no" as groups. This method is rarely used because the individual Senators don't get on the record for the way they voted. The most common and least dramatic vote is done by unanimous consent. Unanimous consent requests are placed on items that are uncontroversial and have been cleared by the leadership, but they can be stopped by the objection of a single present Senator.

The resolution proposed on September 12, 2001, could have been cleared by unanimous consent or a decisively loud voice vote, but the Senators wanted to vote individually through the traditional roll call vote. This vote would be like no other I had seen before or to this day.

All the Senators had just released from their weekly party conferences, so they all reached the Senate chamber on time for the vote. Senator Daschle called for the vote to begin and asked each Senator to vote from his or her desk. Most votes were relatively informal affairs where the Senators stood around for a while talking to one another and voted at their convenience from anywhere on the floor.

The effect of having each Senator sit at their desk and vote was incredible. The Senate chamber was packed as full as I would ever see it. Many pages were busy getting water for the Senators, from the highest-ranking on down the line to the more junior members. A couple of pages were preparing to get a copy of the roll call sheet from the clerk to begin its distribution. Most of the pages, myself included, were finding any small task to do in the Senate chamber just to be there and witness the vote take place. The head pages stood on the rostrum steps with a pen and a roll call sheet, making sure that every Senator was accounted for.

It was an especially easy roll call vote to keep track of because the clerk was able to go down the list once alphabetically and get every Senator's vote. From Senator Akaka of Hawaii to Senator Wyden of Oregon, each Senator was called upon, and each Senator delivered the same vote—"Aye." Within ten minutes 100 of the most powerful people in the world cast a vote for democracy and against the ideology of hatred that had reared its ugly head. The momentum of the vote grew and grew as each Senator added his or her voice to the tally, and I could sense that this united Senate was a great indicator for a united country.

Most of the Senators drifted off the floor as the vote came to a close, and the discussion on the resolution and the terrorist attacks continued. Every Senator used his or her five or ten minutes of speaking time uniquely, but some common themes and messages prevailed.

Many Senators compared the September 11th attacks to the Japanese attack on Pearl Harbor in 1941. The junior Senator from my state made a reference to Pearl Harbor and President Roosevelt's response.

Senator Tim Johnson stated that "not since December 7, 1941, has the United States suffered such a damaging blow on our own soil as the cowardly and hateful terrorist attack our nation sustained on what will become, I am certain, a new day of infamy: September 11, 2001."

I would argue that the date of September 11th, 2001, will take hold of our society in a much more profound way than December 7th, 1941. Pearl

Harbor is a place that will live in infamy because the surprise attack on our
military there is known by its location like the great battles of Yorktown
or Gettysburg. In contrast, the terrorist attacks on September 11th, 2001,
were not limited to one geographic setting, and they targeted civilians in
a way never before seen. Our society has found no other way to describe
these events than by using the date, and it has become so prevalent that
adding the year to clarify is not necessary at all. Even the common short-
hand of "9/11" brings graphic images and strong feelings to mind.

My grandparents' generation was rallied to the cause of freedom on
December 7, 1941—Pearl Harbor. My parents were small children when
another key generational pivot point occurred on November 22, 1963—the
Kennedy assassination. My parents and grandparents went on to pay any
price and bear any burden until November 9, 1989—the fall of the Berlin
Wall. My generation was given its great task on September 11th—no year
necessary, and that's why it is a *date* that lives in infamy. I find it to be
no coincidence that the only other date that holds this power is July 4th, a
date that has come to symbolize the great potential of man through liberty
and democracy.

The Senators also brought great news from their home states regarding other Americans pitching in to help those hit by the terrorists. While
only the East Coast was attacked on September 11th, all Americans from
sea to shining sea were asking what they could do to help. Republican Bill
Frist, who later became Senate majority leader, was only the junior Senator from Tennessee at the time of the attacks. I remember that he seemed
fairly low on the radar at the time, but he was definitely well respected and
had a unique medical background. As a heart surgeon, Frist was the only
medical doctor in the U.S. Senate, and his medical background would get
him more attention when issues of bioterrorism came into play.

"The American spirit is alive. Americans are also united in our desire
and willingness to help. Blood banks are overwhelmed with donors. Special response teams from around the country are organizing to help," Frist
said and went on to give an example from his own state. "A medical group
just arrived from Tennessee to assist at the Pentagon."

At the end of the day, we were all exhausted, but it was a good feeling. We knew that our energy was being spent well to do our small part in keeping the Senate functioning. After that day of speeches, I could see that our government was coming together to strike back at the terrorists with a united effort. Our commitment to justice would not waver. Our duty to the preservation of freedom would be fulfilled.

Senator Chuck Hagel (R-NE) finished his speech with a simple message: "Yesterday the world changed for every American. What those responsible for these barbaric acts will come to learn is that our resolve has not."

The other Senate pages and I could feel that the world had changed for us. In our minds, our workplace went from a tourist site to a possible terrorist target after just one day that will live in infamy. Our job went from a necessary function of the U.S. Senate to a necessary part of the government's response to the largest attack ever on our home soil. The Senators we worked for dropped any level of partisanship from September 10th and united as Americans first on September 12th.

Senator Hagel was right that the world had changed for each of us, and in that situation, the entire Senate's message of a solid resolve in the face of terrorism was what we needed to hear. We Senate pages and our generation as a whole needed to hear from the leadership of the country that they would see this task through to its end. The morale of the American public would play a critical role in this new kind of war. Leaders cannot send mixed messages or take wavering positions if the goal is to preserve the clear message of freedom and crush the untenable position of the terrorists.

All 100 Senators spoke with the needed clarity and conviction in the days after September 11th. They combined their efforts to send that message of resolve to the world through a unanimous roll call vote just one day after the attacks. For the Senate pages, September 13th would test our resolve yet again with its own challenges. It would also serve as an important personal milestone and reminder of our young age, as I would celebrate my 17th birthday.

One thing was crystal clear after September 12th, though. From the 16-year-old pages to the 98-year-old Senator Strom Thurmond (R-SC), we were united in a purpose greater than any one of us individually.

Chapter 7
Happy 17th Birthday

"Well, do you feel any older?"

I'm sure everyone gets asked this somewhat trite question on their birthdays, but I actually did feel older. I had grown up more in the first two weeks of September than I ever thought possible. Our proctors at Webster Hall kept track of all of our birthdays and planned little celebrations in the evening. I shared my birthday with another page, so we had a joint celebration that evening.

Jen Cohen and I both date back to September 13, 1984. She was the head page for my work group on the Senate floor. We became close friends from working and studying together, and I guess the birthday connection didn't hurt either. We joked that day about going to an R-rated movie together, since that was about the only privilege that came with turning 17 years old. Ours was the first birthday to be celebrated for our page class, so the proctors' party was a nice surprise.

We had another big day to get through before any celebrations could take place. September 13th was a Thursday, and the Senators wanted to get a lot done and make Friday a shorter day. The Senate often holds "pro forma" sessions on Mondays or Fridays. A pro forma session occurs when the Senate convenes for just a moment as a formality and then adjourns again for the day. The Senate does this instead of going into a normal recess because of a provision that prohibits either house of Congress from being in recess for a certain number of days while the other house is in session. A pro forma Monday or Friday also makes the weekends longer for the Senators who wish to return to their home states. It puts a lot of pressure on everyone to get work done on Thursdays, and this day was no exception.

The Senate began as it had the day before, with a long list of Senators who wanted to speak on the terrorist attacks. Then it moved on to an appropriations bill. The bill would provide funding to the Departments of Commerce, Justice, and State, as well as the Judiciary. Senator Ernest "Fritz" Hollings (D-SC) and Senator Judd Gregg (R-NH) would be on the floor most of the day managing the debate and procedure on the legislation.

The Senate would get through various amendments to the bill, as well as the final passage of the legislation, on my birthday. During one of the roll call votes that day, I headed down to the subway system underneath the Capitol. Some of the Senators had already voted, but we were waiting on some others. My job would be to call up to the Democratic cloakroom whenever I saw a Democratic Senator on the way up to the Senate Chamber. Any other Senators who weren't accounted for would have to be tracked down by another page, so it was important that I made the others aware which Senators were already on their way.

I walked out of the elevator at the basement level and went down an escalator to the level where the two trams ran. One would bring the Senators with offices in the Russell Building, and the other would bring the Senators with offices in the Hart or Dirksen buildings. I had a roll call list of Democratic Senators with me, so I checked off a few names as I saw them get off their tram and head for the Senate chamber. I then went over to a phone and called up to the cloakroom with the information. I would do this a couple more times before something strange began to unfold.

As I waited for another tram to come to a stop underneath the Capitol, I looked back toward the escalator and the set of elevators. I noticed a few people rushing off the elevators and down the escalator. They didn't stop to wait for one of the trams to take them to an office building, but kept running down the walkway that leads to the Russell Building. It clearly wasn't just a few people in a hurry to get to a meeting because I looked back and saw a flood of staffers coming down the escalator and adjacent staircases.

I had no idea what was going on, and I got the same tensed-up feeling in my chest as I had while evacuating just two days earlier. It's amazing how one's mind can process so many terrible scenarios in just a few moments of time. My fear and confusion was multiplied because I was alone. Luckily, the tram from the Hart and Dirksen buildings was coming to a stop next to me. I saw two other pages getting off, so I was no longer alone in this mess. Adam Anthony, one of my roommates, and Jason Frerichs, a fellow South Dakotan, approached me, wondering if I knew what was going on. I explained that I had been tracking some Senators for the vote. "And then this started," I said, pointing to the staffers coming down the stairs and past the three of us.

We found the nearest Capitol Police officer. We were about to approach her to try to get some answers on what was happening, but two Senators got to her first. Adam, Jason, and I hung back, trying to listen to the Senators' conversation with the officer. We watched Senators Carl Levin and Rick Santorum (R-PA) as they tried to understand the situation. I looked to my roommate Adam with what must have been a worried expression. He responded with a witty comment that put me at ease to a certain degree.

"That's Senator Levin there," he said. "He's chairman of Armed Services. If he's not scared, we've got nothing to worry about."

Adam was right, of course. The two Senators were speaking calmly with the Capitol Police officer about a precautionary evacuation. Both Santorum and Levin looked a little annoyed at the inconvenience, but neither showed any fear or apprehension. I had to laugh a little at Adam's thought process and rationale, but it turned out to be a good way to look at the situation. Each of us had grown accustomed to recognizing the Senators and knowing their leadership status, or lack thereof. When Adam saw Senator Levin, he understood that no Capitol Police officer would stand there and talk with him if he was in real, immediate danger; instead, they would recognize the Senators and tell them to get to a safe place immediately.

We were comforted that the Senators didn't seem worried, but we still didn't know exactly what the extent of the situation was. After a minute of conversation with the Capitol Police, Senator Levin turned and followed the rest of the crowd down the pathway to the Russell Building. Senator Santorum turned away from the officer as well, made eye contact with the three of us, and waved us over to follow him.

He explained that the Capitol complex was being evacuated because an unknown package or box was being investigated. As he led the way to the Russell Building, the Senator asked us how we were holding up in these tough days. We proudly responded that we were doing well and that we were enjoying our jobs.

We stayed with Santorum and walked through the Russell Building. As we stepped outside into the fresh air, I saw a handful of Senators who had already evacuated standing outside of the Russell Building. Senator Ted Kennedy (D-MA) was there playing with his dog! This sight definitely reassured me that we were dealing with a false alarm on this occasion. All the Senators stood around talking to other Senators and their staff members. Everyone seemed to be waiting for the "all clear" sign to head back in and get to work. I expected to simply say a quick goodbye to Senator Santorum, but he waved us on to stay with him.

He wanted to make sure that we got back with the rest of our Senate page group. We assumed that our group would evacuate to the east of the Capitol toward the Supreme Court Building. With this information, the Senator led the way around to the other side of the Russell Building. He guided us to the east side of the Capitol until we could see the rest of our group. We thanked him for his help, and he just smiled and thanked us for our work.

Santorum was one of the many Senators who would go out of his way to make sure that the pages were doing all right through the tough weeks ahead. The Republican pages enjoyed Santorum, especially for the sweets that he left in his desk. Santorum's place on the Senate floor was unique because his desk was the "candy desk" at the time. The desk in the middle of the back row on the Republican side is always stocked with candy by the

Senator who occupies the desk. Since Senator Santorum is from Pennsylvania, he made sure that there was plenty of candy from a town called Hershey! The Democrats have their own desk stocked with candy, but it isn't a Senator's desk. It is a staff desk up against the front wall of the chamber, and I witnessed its frequent visitors from the rostrum steps. I remember Senator Byron Dorgan of North Dakota taking a piece of candy from the desk, then approaching the Senate pages. Dorgan joked that we were supposed to look away when the Senators took candy.

Just as we joined the rest of the pages, the signal was given that we could return to the Capitol. I made my way back to the Senate chamber with Jason. As we stepped off the floor and stood in the entryway of the Democratic cloakroom, Senator Joe Biden approached us.

Biden stopped and asked us if we were doing all right through all the drama of the last few days. We replied that we were doing well. I'm sure I would have said that I was doing well to any Senator who asked, regardless of how I really felt, and maybe Biden sensed this. He looked us over a little bit in an effort to judge for himself how we were doing. Biden is a fairly tall gentleman, so he looked down a few inches to make eye contact with us. He put his right arm out and placed a strong hand around me and onto my opposite shoulder. The Senator nodded his head slowly as if he had just confirmed in his head what he wanted to say.

He reassured us that the Capitol was a safe place to be and that the Senators were going to take the necessary steps to respond to terrorist attacks. Then he said something that has stuck with me as a combination of a simple statement of fact and an incredible personal challenge.

"This is the beginning of the end of terrorism," said the Chairman of the Foreign Relations Committee to a farm boy and a small-town kid from South Dakota.

I looked up at him and understood the strength of his statement. I knew a little bit about Joe Biden before I came to Washington, but now I had seen him handle a lot of the Senate's business in the wake of the terrorist attacks. I could see his age and experience in his graying, nearly white hair, but more importantly, I could see a passion and devotion in his eyes to this cause of ending terrorism. I simply believed what he said must be true. He knew a lot about America and the world around us, and he understood the gravity of his statement. Biden believed in the notion that we were at the beginning of an historic effort, and I believed in him and the rest of the Senators.

Jason and I conveyed our understanding with a "Yes, sir." Biden patted me on the shoulder a couple of times and withdrew his arm from around my back. The Senator made his way into the cloakroom with a smile on his face. That's when I realized that his comment was also a challenge to me, Jason, and our whole generation. He would be able to provide some leadership in the Senate at the outset of this challenge, but the end of terrorism would not come quickly. While this 107th Congress and President Bush would point us in the right direction, I knew that it would have to be my generation that would take up the task of ending terrorism.

I got the feeling that Biden's statement could almost be split in half in a new conversation. He would be able to say "this is the beginning," but I would have to finish his sentence by saying, "of the end of terrorism." I took the personal challenge that seriously.

Of course, acts of a terrorist nature may never end, just as individual crimes of murder and robbery will persist. Individuals with free will can always attack buildings or civilians, especially if they are willing to give up their own lives in the process. The goal must be to end terrorism as a plausible path to political reform. Victory in the War on Terror will come as groups like al-Qaeda realize that the only legitimate changes in society come through the democratic process. We can and will win this new kind of war by showing potential terrorists that freedom and democracy illuminate the path of human destiny instead of fear and violence.

Biden was now past us and into the cloakroom, and I made eye contact with Jason. We looked at each other with wide eyes that expressed the unbelievable nature of our newest experience. We nodded to each other and headed in opposite directions to complete some tasks previously interrupted by the second evacuation to hit the Capitol in three days.

My first chance to think about what an amazing birthday it had been would come after work was done and I was walking home from the Hart Building to Webster Hall. Fittingly enough, it was a day of great, bipartisan memories. I knew that the kindness of Republican Rick Santorum during the evacuation and the personal conversation with Democrat Joe Biden afterwards would stay with me the rest of my life.

After changing into some comfortable clothes, I found the birthday girl, Jen Cohen. We had a few laughs together and reconfirmed that we would be going to an R-rated movie together the next weekend that would work. We started to pull out some physics homework up in the second floor dayroom, but then we noticed the television, which was tuned to C-SPAN2. The Senate was still going strong. The remaining Senate pages from the other work groups moved around on the television screen. All of us gathered around the TV and pointed at the pages sitting on the rostrum until we figured out who was who.

Someone commented that it was past 8:00 p.m. This was important to us because if the Senate stayed in session past 9:00 p.m., none of our homework would be due the next day. If the Senate stayed in session past 10:00 p.m., we would have no school at all the next day. For Jen and me, it was our birthday, and we were willing to chance it. We stopped doing our homework and decided to relax for a while. We watched some TV, flipping back to C-SPAN2 during commercials to make sure the Senate was still chugging along. None of us had all that much homework left, so it was worth the risk to actually get some solid down time for once.

As the clock struck 9:00 p.m., Jen and I got a birthday present from the U.S. Senate in the form of no homework! While we felt bad for the pages still working, we knew that they were cheering for the Senate to go on even further. The nightmare scenario for all the Senate pages was 8:59 p.m. adjournment, and we had made it past that point. We would all work our fair share of late nights, but it was somewhat rare for the Senate to go past 9:00 p.m. and even rarer for it to go past 10:00 p.m., so we were very thankful for the blessing on this day.

The Senate finally adjourned around 9:40 p.m. We would have school the next day, but it would be pretty slack with none of our homework due. The proctors called all the pages downstairs as they arrived back to the dorm for birthday cake with Jen and me. It was a fun celebration as the late-shift pages came down to the kitchen still in their dress clothes to wish me a happy birthday. The rest of us thanked them for helping to keep the Senate going past 9:00 p.m.!

The proctors even allowed us some more wiggle room on the rules of the dorm that evening. They knew that none of our homework was due and that we had been through a lot the past few days, so they pushed back "separate floors." The separate floors rule went into effect at 10:00 p.m. on school nights, requiring the guys to stay on the second floor and the girls to remain on the main level. Many of us took advantage of the opportunity and gathered in the first floor's dayroom.

We hung out there for a while until we convinced Jay Wright to bring down his guitar and play a few songs. Jay was a great guitar player and a good singer to boot. Jen and I sat in the front row for this unplanned mini-concert. It was another great birthday present, and all the other pages appreciated Jay's music as well.

Jay sang four or five songs before the proctors called us to separate floors. It gave me some time to reflect on the events of the past days, as I had on the shores of Chesapeake Beach, Maryland. We all take stock of our lives at least a little bit on our birthdays. It is a part of the celebration of life and the process of maturing as we age. I remember being so thankful to have been able to make it as far as my 17th birthday. Not yet knowing any specifics of the heroic actions on United Flight 93, I thanked God for giving those passengers the strength to bring down that plane before it could reach Washington, D.C. I knew deep down inside that the Capitol could have been the building still smoldering from a terrorist attack instead of the Pentagon or the World Trade Center. I knew that every birthday and every day could no longer be taken for granted. At the same time, I had very little fear because I could feel a sense of purpose among my group of Senate pages to do our part in responding to the terrorists.

I looked over at Jen and saw that beautiful smile of hers as she watched Jay play the guitar. I could tell that Jen had had a great birthday, and I was happy for her. I could feel that I had grown up a lot in just the past couple of days because my own happiness was much more dependent on the happiness of others around me. I think the same was true of many of the other pages. Any selfish bone in our bodies faded away when we were faced with a challenge too great for us to surmount ourselves. Members of this group frequently asked each other how it was going, and more importantly, we truly listened for the response. Many pages would do plenty of favors for other pages without them even having to ask. That evening the bond grew stronger and stronger until Webster Hall was no longer a dormitory for Senate pages, but a home for a large family.

From that day on, a simple gesture from one of the other pages, like a smile from Jen or a conversation about South Dakota with Jason and Katie, would give me more happiness than I could ever achieve on my own.

Over the next several days, we would receive many compliments from Senators in personal conversations. Some Senators even mentioned us while addressing the chamber. Senator Mark Dayton (D-MN) gave a tribute to the pages on September 19, 2001. He came out into the lobby and gathered any of the pages who were around and asked us all to stand on the Senate floor while he addressed the body.

Senator Dayton was one of the favorite Senators of all the pages, especially the Democratic pages. He would always stop to talk with us when passing through the lobby, and he was one of the more entertaining presiding officers. As the most junior member of the U.S. Senate, he had to serve as presiding officer frequently. Dayton had been in the Senate for only a few months, so he was still a little rusty on parliamentary procedure. He would confer with the parliamentarian frequently to make sure he knew what he was doing. Dayton took it all in stride and made fun of himself to the pages by telling us that he was in the "remedial course" on parliamentary procedure. A little self-deprecating humor can go a long way, and we appreciated all his efforts to make us feel like valued members in the Senate family.

Another great example of Dayton's sense of humor came about on a late night of work a few weeks after the terrorist attacks. The Senators were scheduled for three or four straight votes to finish the day, so they were encouraged to stick around the Senate chamber to make the process go as quickly as possible. In between votes, many Senators went to their respective cloakrooms to watch a college football game on television. It was hilarious to hear the cheers and boos coming from the cloakrooms in response to the events of the game while sitting on the rostrum and watching the Senate conduct its business. Once, when I went back to the cloakroom to get some water for a Senator, Senator Dayton happened to be near the water cooler. As I filled the glass, a huge cheer erupted from the Senators on the other side of the room. Dayton turned to me and said, "Well, either we just caught bin Laden, or there was a touchdown!"

With his light-hearted comment, Dayton provided incredible insight on the life of a U.S. Senator at the time in two ways. First, he humanized the Senators. Dayton's humor, combined with the other Senators' fairly rambunctious behavior, showed that the Senators are just like other people who like to have fun and watch football games. At the same time, I could also see that finding Osama bin Laden and responding to the terrorist attacks were always on these people's minds. Even the off-the-cuff, humorous comments of those days were laced with the common resolve to bring justice to the terrorists.

On September 19, Dayton sought recognition to speak after all the pages had joined him on the floor. The Senator stood at his desk and spoke about the importance of our work and the importance of our return to work after two evacuations in a single week.

"I rise today to pay tribute to our pages, who serve us day after day with extraordinary dedication—as do all of our staff—but especially for their exemplary performance last week. They continued their service on the Senate floor in the midst of crisis that had even adults in some alarm," Dayton said with the tone of a proud parent. "Not only did they return to their work after the horrific events of last Tuesday, September 11, but... they are once again assembled, and are working hard on our behalf.

"I ask unanimous consent that their names be printed in the Record. I wish to pay tribute on behalf of all the Senate to them for their dedication and their courage. They are truly outstanding young Americans," Dayton concluded.

It was great to see a U.S. Senator take the time to thank a group of kids who could really get lost in the shuffle or taken for granted under most circumstances. It was now apparent that our resilience over the last couple of weeks had not only been noticed but had inspired at least this one U.S. Senator. It was an amazing feeling to know that we had had a positive effect on the Senators who had been inspiring us from the beginning.

While the public praise from a U.S. Senator boosted our confidence, it didn't go to our heads or inflate any egos. We knew we had a job to do, and we would continue to serve the Senate with modesty. We knew that any dedication or courage that we had inside of us would have been moot had United Flight 93 hit the Capitol. As I learned more and more about the heroes of Flight 93, my belief that they had saved the Capitol and possibly my life grew strong. Receiving praise from various Senators made us all feel great, but we could only pat each other on the back for a moment or two before we thought of our true heroes and were humbled.

Chapter 8
The Lessons of United 93

American soldiers first saw battle in World War I in 1917 with trench warfare in France. The Pacific theatre opened up for the U.S. in World War II with Pearl Harbor, and the Americans took to the beaches of Normandy to liberate France in the European theatre. The first battle of what may come to be known as World War III took place thousands of feet in the air over Pennsylvania on a commercial aircraft.

With the exception of Pearl Harbor, each of these initial efforts by Americans could be considered a victory. The addition of U.S. soldiers to WWI broke the stalemate and brought about the defeat of Germany. The U.S. suffered many casualties on D-day, but the invasion eased pressure on the Soviets on the Eastern front and eventually led to the fall of Hitler. While the attack on Pearl Harbor was clearly a tactical loss for the U.S., President Roosevelt mobilized the military quickly enough to counter the Japanese and eventually win strategic battles in an island-hopping campaign all the way across the Pacific Ocean.

The first battle of the War on Terror in the air over Pennsylvania was a tactical victory for the U.S., but the key differences are glaring. American civilians on board a civilian aircraft were faced with chilling information. A new kind of enemy had presented itself. These enemies would not be wearing military uniforms on an open battlefield or limit their attacks to military targets. Instead, these cowardly enemies would disguise them-

selves as civilians and attempt to destroy any target of value—military, political, or civilian.

The story of the plane crashing in Pennsylvania will forever be a part
of me. It touched the lives of all my friends serving as Senate pages because we happened to be in the political target of the day—the Capitol. It
is a target that some may have forgotten about, since the Pentagon and
the Twin Towers have become the main sites synonymous with the attack. Speculation about the fourth target being the White House is hard
to believe because of the nearly impossible nature of hitting the relatively
low-lying, small target. The Capitol was the symbol of our democracy that
was in jeopardy that day, but luckily, it survived.

Just imagine the damage to the American psyche if the dome of the
Capitol had been obliterated. The additional carnage of another commercial airplane would now be topped with the lives of our nation's congressional leadership and other civilians in the building. Those pictures of the
dome in the background of all the news stations would now be obsolete.
Next time you watch the news, take note of how many times you see a real
shot or a graphic of this symbol of democracy. You would surely have seen
it countless times on September 10th, but September 12th could have been
a different story.

This symbol touches on the true nature of the war we currently fight.
The psychological battles we all wage in our minds play as important a role
as the precision air strikes in Afghanistan and Iraq. The loss of the building where the people's representatives make the laws would have been a
severe blow to each and every American. Luckily, we can thank the passengers of United 93 for their heroism in winning the single biggest psychological victory for the American people that day.

Clearly, heroism by rescuers at the Pentagon and in New York also
provided a psychological victory by showing bravery in the face of terrorism, but United 93 holds a special place in my heart. Of course, I am a bit
biased in the sense that I believe those passengers saved my life or, at the
very least, the building I happened to be in on that terrible morning. My

connection to those heroes is personal, but everyone who has ever been on an airplane can relate in a certain way.

It seems that a random sampling of Americans was chosen to be on that particular flight. I like to think that it was a representative sample and that most Americans would have done what needed to be done. The heroes of United 93 were faced with information that made their hijacking different than most hijackings any of them had ever heard of before. This was not a situation where their captors would land the plane and negotiate for some kind of ransom; this was a suicide mission with an end target of more value than the individual aircraft.

We have all asked ourselves, "Could I bring myself to fight to regain a plane, knowing that the terrorists might crash it on purpose or explode it with a bomb?" Today, I would definitely answer in the affirmative. I am confident that 95% of Americans understand what is truly at stake now in an aircraft hijacking situation. That is why I honestly believe that no terrorist cell will be able to pull off a similar attack as long as American passengers are willing and able to counterattack.

The problem comes when that question poses itself more specifically. "If I had been on that plane on that day, would I have fought back?" I would like to think so, but it is hard to know the true fear and confusion that would have been on that plane. In hindsight, we can all understand that the passengers made the correct decision and executed that decision quickly with the information they had at hand.

This "random sampling" of Americans included a man who, for me, has personified the whole group of heroes. He gave us the phrase that has come to define all of the passengers' heroism—"Let's Roll!" It was the call to decisive action at the exact time it was needed. It has grown even larger to become the battle cry for the spirit of the entire War on Terror. Todd Beamer may have been just one of a random sampling of Americans who were destined to get on that plane on that morning, but it is men like Todd who make me think a higher power made sure the right Americans for the job were on duty that day.

The collective effort of all the passengers on United 93 surely saved the building I was in on that morning, so I consider all of them to be my own heroes. Nonetheless, I feel an even closer connection with Todd Beamer and his personal story. I never had the honor of meeting this great man, but I feel the duty to honor his memory as if he were a lifelong, personal friend.

My mom gave me the book *Let's Roll!* as an early birthday gift nearly a year after the terrorist attacks. I instantly connected with the author of this book, Todd's wife, Lisa Beamer. Since then I have reread her writing each year around the anniversary of the attacks as a reminder of the real people who fought the first battle in the War on Terror. Todd's story sticks with me because I have learned more about him as a regular person through his wife's book. The subtitle to *Let's Roll!* is *Ordinary People, Extraordinary Courage*, and that really explains it all.

Todd was an average American working hard and raising a young family. At the time of his death, he had two young boys and a daughter on the way. Morgan would be born in January. She will never get to know her father, but she will know that he was a hero who gave his life so others could live. Todd's young boys, David and Andrew, naturally struggled with the concept of death. It was hard for them to grasp the fact that Daddy would never be coming home.

In her book, Lisa shared the pain and sorrow of those dark days in September. It was a pain I could imagine all too well as I knew my family could have been experiencing her exact feelings had any circumstances been different on that fateful day. Reading about her pain in her own words invariably led me to feel enormous amounts of guilt that I survived that wretched day while great husbands, great fathers, great Americans had to die.

The only analogy I have come across to accurately describe the feeling came in Tom Brokaw's book *The Greatest Generation*. Brokaw recounted a story in which a group of four soldiers in a bunker were attacked and one survived by pure chance. The surviving soldier felt an immense amount of guilt that he survived while his comrades next to him perished. On September 11th, the Capitol was that fourth soldier. My Senate page friends and I understand that certain circumstances worked out that day that spared our lives, as well as the building that houses and symbolizes our democracy, and some of us could surely relate to the guilt of that fourth soldier.

One of my fellow pages has yet to read Lisa Beamer's book to this day because she knows that it will be too difficult to get through. The emotions cut deep when you understand the gripping reality of that day. Each time I read *Let's Roll*! the amount of time I feel those pangs of guilt lessens. I have slowly come to terms with the way things worked out that day, and I have grown in my faith in the process. Lisa recounts her own struggle to get through the grieving process and describes how her faith in God helped her.

When she questioned her faith along the way, Lisa referred to a passage in the Bible that shone some light on the bigger picture. Romans 11:33-36 reads, "Oh, the depth of the riches of the wisdom and knowledge of God! How unsearchable his judgments, and his paths beyond tracing out! Who has known the mind of the Lord? Or who has been his counselor? Who has ever given to God, that God should repay him? For from him and through him and to him are all things. To him be the glory forever! Amen."

Upon reading this as part of Lisa Beamer's own troubles, I instantly thought of Senator Robert Byrd. His message on September 10th was essentially the same. Who are we to question an omnipotent and omniscient being? We cannot grasp the knowledge of God's larger plan. We must trust in Him that a purpose will reveal itself.

That may be the hardest part of faith—trust. We must hand over some of the control of our lives to God. That is easier said than done, of course. I like to be in control of all the logistics around me and be "in the know" about events happening later today, next week, and next month. I learned a lesson, though, on September 11th. I can't be in control of everything that happens, how it happens, when it happens, or to whom it happens.

It is a helpless feeling. It is a feeling shared by that fourth soldier in the bunker and by all those in the Capitol that day.

The incredible odds on the survival of the Capitol made it much more apparent to me that a higher power was present that day to hand one victory to the good guys. It isn't quite as simple as the story of the soldiers in the bunker. Given that only one was going to survive, that one soldier had just a 25% shot at being alive. The Capitol was one of four targets as well, but the odds were a bit more complicated.

First, it had only a 25% chance of being the last target of the day. If the Capitol had been in the top three, the passengers would not have learned of the other attacks until it was too late. I would like to assume that the passengers of the other three planes would have attempted to take back their planes if they had been in the same circumstances as United 93. Worse still, if the terrorists had coordinated their timing better, all the planes could have hit their targets within a couple of minutes of one another, and none of the passengers, in all likelihood, would have done a thing.

The chance delay of United 93 for about a half hour before take off would make history. Plenty of war stories are thrown around in which one side wins by a lucky break, like weather or timing. This first battle of the War on Terror would steal a page from these stories in the form of a backed-up runway. These precious minutes would make the difference for Todd Beamer and others to gain knowledge and take action.

All of this knowledge gives me some comfort that a higher power had a purpose for those exact passengers of United 93. The random events of the day seem to carry an underlying purpose, as each event led to another in a perfect example of the Butterfly Effect. Every variable worked out, each building on the others, to give those passengers their opportunity to be heroes. Their counterattack was destined to be the bellwether, demonstrating how to fight this new kind of war successfully. I thank them every day for acting decisively and not squandering that opportunity.

Still, the guilt gets to me every once in a while. I feel a sudden pang when I imagine the final couple of seconds on board United 93. "Why them? Why a field in Pennsylvania? Why not the Senate chamber?" I ask myself in that moment. When reading that chapter in *Let's Roll!* or watching the end of the United 93 movie, those questions blaze through my mind, followed by the image of those left behind—Lisa and little David, Andrew, and Morgan. "Why them? Why is their husband and father gone forever? Why am I still here?" I ask myself.

I have had this feeling enough times that all these questions and emotions rage forward very quickly. I can process it all in an instant now because, although it does get replayed, the debate is over in my head. The last question is always answered with "a purpose." The apparent random nature of that day fades away. The faith that drove Lisa Beamer taught that her husband served a great purpose by saving the lives of others and defeating the terrorists. I have my own trust in God, my own faith, which points to the fact that my purpose in life is still ahead of me. It could be a large purpose or a small one. I don't quite know what it is yet, but there is one being who does, and I'm learning to trust Him more each day.

At the University of Notre Dame, a motto lists three key elements in life—"God, Country, Notre Dame." For all you non-Golden Domers out there, "Notre Dame" can be replaced with what I consider a synonym—family. I see a successful, purpose-driven life as one that strives to serve all three of these elements. Having a sense of purpose sure made getting up at 5:15 a.m. every morning to serve as a Senate page a lot easier!

Todd and the other passengers gave us all a sense of purpose in carrying on their fight in the War on Terror. They also gave us the template for how to fight—take the battle to the enemy. With the knowledge we now have of al-Qaeda, we will not sit, metaphorically, at the back of the plane. We will charge forward and fight the terrorists at locations of our choosing, on our terms, before they can bring the war back to our homeland.

Our nation's leaders modeled Operation Enduring Freedom in Afghanistan with this idea in mind. We had to strike at the heart of al-Qaeda and begin the process of disrupting and eliminating the organization. The liberation of Afghanistan was largely successful because a terrorist haven was replaced with a democratically elected government. Throughout the operations in Afghanistan, American casualties have remained relatively low. Some would argue that a fear of casualties at Tora Bora cost us our best chance of capturing Osama bin Laden, but the overall objective was still achieved. The terrorist network al-Qaeda no longer had a stronghold of territory for planning, training, and executing its evil deeds. Bin Laden and the rest of his henchmen were on the run, and for a time our nation seemed to be united on keeping these extremists on the run.

Iraq became a different story in regard to the unity of our great country. If we look back to our original sense of purpose derived from the heroes of 9/11, we will see that victory in Iraq must be achieved. Operation Iraqi Freedom took the fight to the enemy again with the goal of ousting a terrible dictator with a murderous history and replacing him with a unique type of government in the Arab world—a democracy. I do not propose that the argument of taking the fight to the enemy by itself justified the invasion of Iraq (although I do think the invasion of Iraq was justified in combination with other reasons), but I do believe that completing the mission of standing up a healthy Iraqi democracy that can prevent an al-Qaeda takeover before we stand down does reflect the spirit of our 9/11 heroes.

Let's leave it to the historians to debate whether or not we were right to invade Iraq. The fact is that we are there. And another fact is that al-Qaeda is there. As I will detail in the next chapter, President Bush warned us after 9/11 that this would be a long struggle, and we must continue to show vigilance and patience because Iraq is part of the broader War on Terror.

After the quick fall of Saddam Hussein, the enemies of freedom protracted the battle to resist the shift to liberty. A group of radical sectarians, along with followers of the prominent al-Qaeda leader Abu Musab al-Zarqawi, have attempted to use terror to disrupt the steady drumbeat of democracy. Election after election, the Iraqi people showed that they were choosing the future prosperity that democracy can offer instead of the hopelessness and despair that al-Qaeda would bring. It is now our responsibility to stay the course and see to it that no ground is ceded to the terrorist organization.

If we had listened to some in Congress who must have placed a personal sunset provision on their commitment to the principles we learned on September 11th, we would have abandoned the Iraqi people after helping them for only a couple of years. Yes, this would most likely have saved hundreds of U.S. soldiers' lives, but al-Zarqawi would still be alive. And a living al-Zarqawi means not hundreds but surely thousands of deaths of defenseless Iraqis. In addition, a safe haven for evil in the heart of the Middle East would eventually lead to the violence returning to our own shores. Instead of having only our volunteer military in harm's way, we would be offering up the territory and the innocent population of Iraq to al-Qaeda on a silver platter and again putting our homeland and our civilians in danger.

None of this is consistent with what we have learned in our War on Terror. We must show resilience, and we cannot allow al-Qaeda to control any geographic area for a base of operations. I am confident that the high morale we see among our troops fighting in this new kind of war is a reflection of their understanding of the importance of their mission. I am also confident that my generation understands the need to complete the mission on all fronts.

A couple of generations ago, there may have been similar objectors to the strategy in the Pacific theatre of World War II. The painstaking process of island-hopping through the battles of Coral Sea, Midway, and countless small islands was necessary to put the final pressure on Japan to surrender. Fighting the amazingly determined Japanese soldiers on seemingly worthless pieces of land in the middle of an ocean, our servicemen would suffer in just a few *days* numbers of casualties similar to the number of deaths we have suffered in a few *years* of fighting the determined jihadists in Iraq.

Take a look at a map of the Pacific Ocean and know that the blood of American sailors and marines is on countless islands, from Hawaii all the way to Okinawa. Find the island of Iwo Jima and try to comprehend that we lost more men on this one island in about a month of fighting than we have lost in our entire time in Iraq. Imagine the lunacy of having told our soldiers just to come on home and forget their mission a couple of weeks into that battle, after they had lost many of their friends. We didn't even consider such an option during WWII because we knew what was at stake. Instead of retreating, we claimed that small island in the name of freedom with the classic image of soldiers raising the American flag. Now our mission is to help the Iraqis raise their own flag of democracy and wave it proudly in the face of any terrorist intimidation.

Victory at Iwo Jima is to WWII what victory in Iraq will be to the War on Terror. The same spirit of our grandfathers in WWII is truly present in our time, as demonstrated by ordinary citizens with extraordinary courage. We only need to recapture that spirit and understand what we already know. As the saying goes, everything we need to know we learned in Kindergarten, and our metaphorical Kindergarten in this war was the lesson of 9/11 and United 93.

Lisa Beamer entitled one of her chapters concerning her husband's death "Saying Good-Bye to Todd ... For Now." This title has stuck with me because of its simple message of hope and optimism. Lisa has faith that she will be reunited with her husband again someday in Heaven. Likewise, someday Morgan will be with the father who was taken from her before birth. I look forward to the chance to meet my hero as well. Until then, I will wake up each morning with a sense of purpose given to me by God and by the heroes of United 93.

And America will move forward in its War on Terror with the true spirit of the words of Todd Beamer, "Let's Roll!"

CHAPTER 9
PRESIDENT BUSH
ADDRESSES THE NATION

M r. Speaker, the President of the United States!"
I pushed toward the center aisle of the U.S. House
chamber, along with the rest of the Congressional pages,
to catch a glimpse of the President. All the pages were crammed into the
back of the chamber. The pages serving the U.S. House had already staked
out all the good spots near the center aisle by the time the Senate pages
arrived. Nonetheless, I stood on the tips of my toes and craned my neck to
look for the commander in chief.

The Senate pages had been anticipating this event all day long. It was
September 20, 2001, and President Bush was addressing a joint session of
Congress that evening. The Senate had adjourned earlier that evening, but
we hung out in the lobby and the cloakrooms until it was time to head over
to the other side of the Capitol.

Each of the cloakrooms contained a box of American flag ribbons to
pin on our lapels. Many of the Senators wore them during the President's
speech to the joint session of Congress. Normally, the Senate pages are
only allowed their name tags and official Senate page lapel pins, but those
regulations relaxed in the days after September 11th. I noticed that many
of the Senators (and nearly all of the TV anchors) began wearing American
flag lapel pins after the terrorist attacks. Later in September, Senator Jack
Reed (D-RI) put a basket of these lapel pins in the Democratic cloakroom

for any staffer or page who wanted one. I proudly displayed the American flag on my lapel, compliments of a U.S. Senator, and it is one of my favorite possessions to this day.

The Senators began to gather on the floor of the U.S. Senate sometime after 8:00 that evening. Those Senators in the leadership would be part of the group escorting President Bush into the House chamber. All the rest were milling about the Senate floor, waiting for the green light to head over to the House side of the Capitol. They would walk over together and find their assigned seats, and the pages would follow and stand in the back of the chamber.

I remember being slightly nervous about the joint session. It wasn't because I was afraid of another terrorist attack, although the thought had crossed my mind. I knew the gathering of nearly all the members of Congress, most of the President's cabinet, many Supreme Court justices, and the President of the United States would make a great target. I was not surprised to see Senator Robert Byrd, instead of Vice President Dick Cheney, sitting next to the Speaker of the House while the President spoke. Cheney was, of course, in an undisclosed location for security reasons, but this wasn't the cause for my butterflies.

I felt nervous because I felt that I was almost a direct participant in the incredible event about to take place. President Bush would be the one giving the speech, but I almost had some stage fright myself. This feeling is a testament to our spectacular look at history unfolding before us. We pages would be among the few to have the opportunity to witness first-hand the President giving the most important speech of his life. The President would represent America to the rest of the world. Every word he chose that night would point out the direction in which we were headed as a nation.

Before we could move forward, we needed to be reminded of where we had come from. The Senate pages' journey to the other side of the Capitol would serve this purpose. After the Senators led the way out of the Senate chamber, we lined up and began the march two by two. The busts of the first 20 Vice Presidents of the United States watched over us as we made our way out of the chamber.

As we passed through the rotunda, I glanced up at the dome. The incredible architecture and Constantino Brumidi's frieze "Apotheosis of Washington" rose high above us. Large oil paintings depicting scenes from American history surrounded us at floor level. The presentation of the Declaration of Independence, victorious battles in the Revolutionary War, and the discovery of the Mississippi River are among the pictures. In between the paintings stand the likenesses of some of our greatest Americans carved in stone. Statues of Abraham Lincoln, Thomas Jefferson, and George Washington in his military uniform line the perimeter of the rotunda.

Next we came upon Statuary Hall, where the U.S. House of Representatives met until 1857. The old Hall of the House now holds about one-third of the National Statuary Hall Collection. Each state has the right to enshrine two of their citizens in statue form for display in the Capitol. Sam Houston, Robert E. Lee, and Daniel Webster are among the many immortalized in the collection.

Finally, we entered the current House chamber, where history would be made before our eyes. I took some time to look around and see who was in attendance. From my position in the back of the chamber on the Republican side, I could see the First Lady up in the gallery to my right. British Prime Minister Tony Blair sat to her right, while New York's Mayor Rudy Giuliani and Governor George Pataki sat to her left. I recognized my Congressman, John Thune, in the back row on the floor of the House. Jason and I would approach him after the speech and shake his hand. In the minutes before the speech, the other pages and I were excitedly whispering to each other as we recognized more and more important people in the chamber.

The sergeant at arms of the House bellowed the announcement of the President's entrance. I recognized a familiar face next to him. It was the sergeant at arms of the Senate, Al Lenhardt. Both sergeants at arms would be leading President Bush into the chamber for this joint session of Congress. Following Bush would be the leadership of both houses of Congress.

I saw the top of the President's head go by and cheered loudly. The entire chamber gave the President an enthusiastic and loud welcome. There was something more special than the sights and sounds at this point. As the President of the United States walked to the podium and looked out over his audience, a magical feeling pulsed through the chamber. We were united as never before, and our leader had arrived to lay out the plan to victory. The energy and emotions of the past nine days came out all at once in the enormous cheer of support for the President.

The applause could have carried on nearly forever, but the anticipation of the President's words finally got the best of the audience. At 9:00 p.m. on September 20, 2001, President Bush began the best speech of life.

"In the normal course of events, Presidents come to this chamber to report on the state of the Union," he said. "Tonight, no such report is needed. It has already been delivered by the American people. We have seen it in the courage of passengers, who rushed terrorists to save others on the ground—passengers like an exceptional man named Todd Beamer. And would you please help me to welcome his wife, Lisa Beamer, here tonight."

A standing ovation immediately followed the President's opening lines. Lisa Beamer was in the gallery to the President's right. I had not recognized her before, and I didn't recognize her then. I didn't know her husband's story at the time, but the President's description made it clear that Todd was one of the heroes of Flight 93. I love looking back at this speech to this day knowing that the first person that the President mentions is my personal hero, Todd Beamer. And possibly even more special is the fact that the speech was written and delivered in a way that gave Lisa Beamer the first round of applause.

Lisa stood up from her seat in the gallery to thank the President and the rest of us cheering in the name of her late husband. I could sense her modesty even then as she accepted the applause and sat back down, knowing that her husband was only one of the nation's many recent heroes.

Bush went on to recognize the amazing efforts of rescue workers and the outpouring of support and love from average Americans to those who were grieving. Then he gave a powerful and emphatic statement to the world.

"My fellow citizens, for the last nine days, the entire world has seen for itself the state of our Union—and it is strong," Bush proclaimed, and he received robust agreement from both sides of the aisle with a standing ovation.

"Tonight we are a country awakened to danger and called to defend freedom. Our grief has turned to anger, and anger to resolution. Whether we bring our enemies to justice, or bring justice to our enemies, justice will be done."

It was a clear message to those in the U.S. House chamber, to those Americans watching on television at home, and to the citizens of the world that America would not be a paper tiger. President Bush recognized America's grief and felt the pain of many of the victims' families with whom he had visited throughout that week. He understood the anger pointed at the cowardly attacks, yet he did not call for cold-blooded revenge, but justice. He understood that the American citizens could channel their grief and anger into a united resolve that would bring justice and preserve freedom.

President Bush noted that unity at the top levels of government was already taking hold. He thanked the leaders in Congress by name for their friendship and leadership. Bush thanked the people of the world for an outpouring of support and prayers of sympathy. Citizens from Pakistan, Israel, India, El Salvador, Iran, Mexico, Japan, and Great Britain lost their lives along with Americans on September 11th. The President pledged that he would not forget these citizens that died or the emotional support that foreign countries offered.

British Prime Minister Tony Blair received two standing ovations. The first came as President Bush declared that "America has no truer friend than Great Britain." We have seen this to be true through both kind words and supportive action by Blair and his government. His support in Afghanistan, Iraq, and the War on Terror in general has shown the alliance to be as strong as ever. A country with Great Britain's experience in World

War II under the leadership of Winston Churchill knows the resolve that it takes to win a war where our very existence as a free society is at stake. I can think of no better ally to have in fighting an aggressive war. I can think of no better friend to have in an effort to preserve democracy.

The chamber erupted again two sentences later as Bush thanked Blair for crossing an ocean "to show his unity of purpose with America." Blair stood on both occasions to accept the applause on behalf of his nation. Blair's personal eloquence in making the case to the British people for fighting the War on Terror runs much deeper than a charming British accent. He has stood with President Bush even when this action has gone against public sentiment in Europe, and he gained a renewed sense of purpose after his own country's civilians were attacked in July of 2005.

President Bush called the attacks of September 11th an "act of war" and referenced the similarity to "one Sunday in 1941." Americans knew from the start that this war was different, though. President Roosevelt and the 77th Congress passed a Declaration of War following the Japanese attack on Pearl Harbor. Now President Bush and the 107th Congress had to explain to the American people just who had attacked us and how we could respond.

The President explained that it was not another country that had attacked our cities, but a group of "loosely affiliated terrorist organizations known as al-Qaeda." I recognized the name when the President said it because I had heard it used on the Senate floor in the past couple of days. Most Americans were not familiar with the terrorist group before the President's speech, and very few would have recognized the name before September 11. Because it was a relatively new word to the American lexicon and had to be translated from Arabic, several different spellings of "al-Qaeda" floated around in the weeks after the attacks. The Senate's stenographers picked a spelling and stuck with it. When I delivered some of the Senators' speeches to the stenographers' office in basement of the Capitol, I noticed that they had the name of the terrorist organization written on a chalkboard for reference.

President Bush also introduced the name of Osama bin Laden and condemned the Taliban regime in Afghanistan. The President cited the ridiculous restrictions placed on the people of Afghanistan because of al-Qaeda and the Taliban. Rights and privileges that are taken for granted in our free and liberal societies could not be found at all for the people in Afghanistan. Women could not attend school, and people could be arrested for owning televisions. Religious practices came with dictatorial control, so men could be jailed if their beards were not long enough. It was now clear that the people who attacked us had no concept of liberty. The terrorists and the Taliban government that supported them had an agenda of imposing their extremist beliefs, and freedom was not one of those beliefs.

President Bush made many demands on the Taliban government, including handing over the terrorists residing in Afghanistan. He made it clear that supporting the terrorists was the moral equivalent of being terrorists, so the Taliban would share the fate of al-Qaeda. Everyone in the chamber that evening knew that the Taliban would not comply with America's demands, and military action was on its way. While Bush explained that we would be fighting al-Qaeda and the Taliban, he also conveyed an important message on what we weren't fighting.

As the President pointed out, America looks kindly upon the basic teachings of Islam and welcomes the many millions within the United States who freely practice Islam. While the religion's true teachings are good and peaceful, the terrorists have perverted them for evil and violence. Most of the Muslim world objects to this extreme form of the religion, but America battles not only the terrorists' extreme beliefs, but also negative public perception throughout the Middle East. The War on Terror has become a war of public relations as much as it has been a war of bullets and missiles. Winning the hearts and minds of Muslims might not be easy, but it can be done. The drive toward the values of freedom and democracy exists in all people regardless of religious background. America has to explain the power of civil liberties taken for granted here to people who have known nothing but fear and propaganda. Before we can win hearts and minds to our side, we have to assure Muslims across the world that they are not the ones we wish to fight.

"The terrorists are traitors to their own faith, trying, in effect, to hijack Islam itself," Bush said. "The enemy of America is not our many Muslim friends; it is not our many Arab friends. Our enemy is a radical network of terrorists, and every government that supports them."

Bush also began to make the argument that the terrorists' extremism was on the wrong side of history. Extreme ideologies had threatened freedom before September 11, 2001. America's history, especially over the last century, has been filled with battles against nothing less than evil. Bush emphasized that we would not be deceived by evil disguised as religion. The terrorists' pretenses to piety and their rhetoric that blames America and democracy for the troubles of the world cannot be accepted.

"They are the heirs of all the murderous ideologies of the 20th century. By sacrificing human life to serve their radical visions—by abandoning every value except the will to power—they follow in the path of fascism, and Nazism, and totalitarianism. And they will follow that path all the way, to where it ends: in history's unmarked grave of discarded lies," Bush said.

We all knew that Osama bin Laden, the terrorist network al-Qaeda, and the countries that supported their activities were now pitted against the free world. We also knew that we had great allies in Europe like Tony Blair and Arab and Muslim friends that could help our effort of defending freedom. Black and white, good and evil, right? Some people will always find comfort by creating shades of gray, but we can't lose our resolve debating what constitutes "a little bit evil." When we are fighting enemies who will sacrifice their own lives to fly planes into buildings in New York or kill innocent commuters in London, the nuances and the shades of gray are harder to find.

If you put your nose up against a big screen television, you can see individual pixels that show some subtleties and nuances of color, but you have no idea what's going on over the screen as a whole. When you step back a few feet and look at the screen, the individual pixels matter less than the bigger picture. In terms of the War on Terror, that bigger picture shows freedom fighting for its very existence against an enemy that knows nothing but the power that comes from fear. And maybe if you step back a bit further or think a bit harder, you realize that if you were watching this television in Afghanistan with the Taliban and al-Qaeda in control, you would be thrown in jail!

Still, many people will want the comfort and compromise that comes with the shades of gray. Many of those people will bring up legitimate points and show some individual pixels in our big picture that need to be improved. Our democracy allows for a sufficient dialogue for the exact purpose of improving our country. The trouble will come from those that do not understand the concept of this new kind of war. Their resolve will waver when we suffer casualties, when the war turns into years instead of months, and when the morality of our mission is questioned even by those with no morals. The President knew that this war would be different. It would not be conventional like meeting Hitler's army on the battlefield. It would not be like the Cold War, during which our democracy and free market outpaced and overcame the inherent flaws in communism. We would now have to be proactive in a new way, which would open us up for criticism, but Bush began to make his case.

"This war will not be like the war against Iraq a decade ago, with a decisive liberation of territory and a swift conclusion. It will not look like the air war above Kosovo two years ago, where no ground troops were used and not a single American was lost in combat...Americans should not expect one battle, but a lengthy campaign, unlike any other we have ever seen," Bush warned his audience.

Bush mentioned diplomacy, intelligence, financial influence, and military actions as parts of the overall effort of fighting the terrorist organization. He announced the creation of the Office of Homeland Security, which has now become the Department of Homeland Security. Bush also announced the selection of Pennsylvania Governor Tom Ridge to lead the new agency. Every tool at our disposal needed to be sharpened and pointed in the right direction. Governor Ridge's job would involve a massive reorganization of all agencies involved in protecting the homeland. Two oceans had protected our homeland for many years, but our geography was no longer enough.

Ridge was a popular governor at the time and seemed like a great choice to start the effort of homeland security off on the right foot. He received a good amount of applause from those in the chamber, but the loudest applause would come later in the speech when the leaders of New York were mentioned.

Everyone knew that Governor George Pataki and Mayor Rudy Giuliani were in attendance because they were seated next to Laura Bush, Prime Minister Blair, and Governor Ridge. Everyone knew that their time would come to be recognized, and all the energy and support for New Yorkers was waiting to burst. When the President did mention them by name, the chamber roared with great admiration. I remember it as the loudest cheer because I could actually feel it rumble in my ears. Giuliani's leadership, especially, had rallied the New Yorkers to dig deep to find the necessary resilience. Both men were Republicans, but political parties didn't matter at this time in New York either. They led fellow Americans and New Yorkers through the dark days with optimism and without partisanship.

America would not only rebuild New York and bulk up its defenses at home; it would also bring the fight to the terrorist organization to disrupt their activities before they could reach our homeland.

"And tonight, a few miles from the damaged Pentagon, I have a message for our military: Be ready. I've called the Armed Forces to alert, and there is a reason. The hour is coming when America will act, and you will make us proud," said the commander in chief.

It would not be just the American government and the American military called into action in the coming weeks. President Bush called on the world to join the effort, saying that a terrorist attack on one country is an attack on all countries. Allies will prove essential throughout the War on Terror, and Bush challenged every country to see the big picture and make clear decisions. Bush asked every country in every region to decide whether "you are with us, or you are with the terrorists." The rest of the world would make those decisions, and we would be left with many allies and a handful of hostile regimes.

President Bush understood the rationale for coming to America's aide and combining forces to fight the evil that had presented itself. He made a memorable statement that combined simple logic, mild eloquence, and a Texas-style clincher.

"The civilized world is rallying to America's side. They understand that if this terror goes unpunished, their own cities, their own citizens may be next. Terror, unanswered, can not only bring down buildings, it can threaten the stability of legitimate governments," Bush said, then paused, shook his head, and placed a clinched fist on the podium. "And you know what—we're not going to allow it."

The President's folksy style made it feel as though he could have delivered a line like this in a coffee shop in Ohio or a town hall meeting in Nebraska. Bush knew how to speak to the average American. Many Americans simultaneously look up to the President and First Lady with the utmost respect and want to invite George and Laura over for the family barbecue. While he can be the butt of many jokes, rational people understand that Bush is an intelligent person surrounded by even more intelligent people. We can only hope that the terrorists "misunderestimate" the President as much as some of his political opponents have.

I personally believe that this was the best speech of Bush's first term, and it may even edge out his second inaugural address. It can be looked at as a guiding document for the War on Terror which Bush has consistently followed. While it is a great speech, it does not contain his greatest line from this time period.

That line came when he was standing at Ground Zero in New York City on September 14, 2001. He was speaking to a group of New Yorkers who would be clearing the rubble on which they stood. As he spoke some unremarkable comments into a megaphone, someone in the crowd yelled, "We can't hear you!" The President responded with, "I can hear you. The rest of the world hears you, and the people who knocked these buildings down will hear from all of us soon." The crowd went nuts with excitement because they knew it was the truth.

It is Bush's most powerful line because it was an unscripted comment from one man to another. It was an assurance that Bush would do what needed to be done. He was giving his word on hallowed ground that he could hear the call for justice from the American people, and he pledged that all of them together would bring that justice to the terrorists. It was Bush at his best—unscripted, with a small audience and a big subject.

Bush did have some great lines in his September 20th speech. Near the end came one that looked to the future and could even be read as a preview of his second inaugural address. He spoke to any self-doubt within his fellow citizens on what was to come.

"After all that has just passed—all the lives taken, and all the possibilities and hopes that died with them—it is natural to wonder if America's future is one of fear. Some speak of an age of terror. I know there are struggles ahead and dangers to face," Bush said. Then he went on to explain the enormous opportunity in front of us. "[T]his country will define our times, not be defined by them. As long as the United States of America is determined and strong, this will not be an age of terror; this will be an age of liberty, here and across the world."

This "age of liberty" has to be fought for and defended. While our country has found freedom, we have also found that freedom is not free. As the costs in the War on Terror become real, the strength of our resolve will be tested. The President emphasized the need for a steady resolve among all citizens well after September 2001.

"We will not tire, we will not falter, and we will not fail," Bush said. "Even grief recedes with time and grace. But our resolve must not pass."

President Bush also put the commitment and the responsibility on his shoulders to take up this fight. A handful of years have passed, but we must all realize that he is the only human being to know what it is like to be President of the United States in a post-9/11 world. He carried the sorrow and anger of an entire country for nine days before addressing Congress. He had visited New York and the Pentagon, and he had met with the victims' families. A good democracy will always question its leaders, but good leaders will have answers that come from personal understanding and experience. Bush has that understanding and experience. From the moment Andy Card entered a Florida classroom to tell the President that America was under attack, Bush has been a leader with a clear mission.

"I will not forget this wound to our country or those who inflicted it. I will not yield; I will not rest; I will not relent in waging this struggle for freedom and security for the American people," Bush told the joint session of Congress.

Bush knew that his chapter in history would be dominated by the effort to end terrorism. He knew that he would be judged by his fellow citizens now and by countless generations in the future. He could not predict the way this new kind of war would work. No battle plan survives first contact with the enemy completely intact. We would have to be flexible and resilient. We would have to be patient and strong.

"The course of this conflict is not known, yet its outcome is certain. Freedom and fear, justice and cruelty, have always been at war, and we know that God is not neutral between them," Bush said, and a round of applause followed.

This may have been the best statement of the evening. Bush was humble yet confident. He acknowledged that this war would be difficult and would include many variables, but it would be won by the forces of freedom and justice. Moral relativism will not win this war because God is not neutral between good and evil. The big picture is clear, and there is no other option but to win this conflict decisively.

The 41-minute speech ended with the American people more united than anyone could have imagined less than a year before. The fall of 2000 had held a bitter presidential election that essentially ended in a statistical tie in Florida. The country was divided into camps of Democrats or Republicans and supporters of Gore or Bush. The fall of 2001 showed the true strength of the United States. The citizens united as Americans first and supported the person who was the President of the United States, regardless of party affiliation.

Many remember the hug that President Bush and Senator Daschle shared as Bush began to leave the House chamber that evening. They were the two people I looked up to the most in the political world, and now the whole country was looking to them for leadership. When the War on Terror is won, we can thank these two men and their cooperation at the outset. When terrorism is no longer seen as an option to bring about change, Democrats and Republicans will be thanked, and Bush and Daschle will be among the names mentioned.

They would have many political battles regarding the specific actions taken in carrying out this new war, and they would continue to throw punches on separate, domestic issues. Bush would barnstorm the country a year later and gain control of the U.S. Senate in the midterm election. In what would require another full book to explain, Daschle went on to lose his own Senate seat to John Thune during an intense political season in South Dakota. Politically, it may seem that President Bush won, but history will look less at one election in South Dakota than at the big picture. In the long run, Americans won't care that President Bush defeated some Democratic rivals. Americans will care about what Republicans and Democrats did to win what may eventually be defined as World War III.

Both Daschle and Bush knew that political battles were on the horizon. On this evening, though, there was only time for friendship and a renewed commitment to the security of the United States. The hug in the House chamber signaled a bond that had to overcome partisanship. The President pushed forward to use the military in Afghanistan. Senator Daschle made sure the Congress approved the necessary funding and strongly encouraged the President to keep the Congress informed of all military action. An agenda was pushed through the Congress that included increasing airline security and expanding the tools available to law enforcement for cracking down on terrorists.

These actions may have been simple, and maybe any leaders could have accomplished them. Maybe a President Al Gore could have worked with a Majority Leader Trent Lott, but that point is moot. Just as Bush was the only one to know what it was like to be President on September

11th, Daschle was the only one to know what it was like to be the leader of a majority opposition party to that President.

American history is filled with these elements of chance, destiny, divine intervention, or whatever you may choose to call it. Our war for independence could have been lost at countless points, and the Confederacy had some chances to win the Civil War. The explicit wording of our Constitution, decided on over two centuries ago, has led to laws and decisions on laws that could never have been imagined by the original writers of the document. The Cuban missile crisis put the entire world on the edge of disaster, but somehow the leaders of the two superpowers resolved the issue. A boy from Aberdeen, South Dakota grew up to be the leader of the U.S. Senate. A boy from Midland, Texas grew up to be President of the United States. America needed both of them, and they needed each other.

The embrace between Bush and Daschle on the floor of the House signaled an understanding that a post-9/11 world needed a new mindset. The partisan divide needs to be closed when it comes to the War on Terror, and we need to concentrate on winning rather than on assigning credit or blame. Many would argue that the hug was not a sign of a permanent change in mindset but only a "honeymoon" period for the President. Vicious fights over judicial nominees, social security reform, and tax reform show that domestic issues can still smack of partisanship. Better evidence is the partisan divide over the decision to take the fight to Iraq. Many with more experience than I have could argue effectively that Washington is more partisan now than ever.

I agree that some will cling tightly to the past in which partisanship leads to short-term gains. Some find it easier and more comfortable to disagree with the other party for the sake of disagreement. Some also find it easy to write off any conflict in Washington as a partisan struggle. These are troubling times, and politics does play a role, but there is an understanding among rational leaders that more is at stake than political elections.

My experiences and gut feelings tell me that there has been a change in Washington since the fall of 2001. It may have been more pronounced in a honeymoon period, but underneath the surface of political posturing lie plenty of good people working hard to protect America. The heroes of my generation will not be remembered as Democrats or Republicans. People who understand history and look forward to a future of democracy know that short-term political gains mean little. Long-term results like those outlined in Bush's second inaugural address come only with steady progress from a resolved group of people.

No one remembers whether Lincoln had the political capital to increase domestic spending on a social program in 1864. He preserved the Union and ended slavery.

No one remembers whether President Roosevelt got an appellate court nominee he wanted on the bench in 1944. He stormed Normandy and defeated Hitler.

Few will care that Ronald Reagan was a huge political success and won the 1984 election by a landslide. The world cares that the Cold War was ended.

My great-great-grandchildren won't care that the Republicans gained seats in 2002 and that Senator Daschle was defeated in 2004. They will care about the result of the War on Terror. They will study the history books that show how my generation brought the fight to the terrorists and not only secured freedom at home, but also introduced it to the Middle East.

Maybe they'll learn about that hug, too.

Chapter 10
Kids will be Kids

O n September 27, 2001, the Senate pages from South Carolina returned home. The four pages had been selected by Senator Strom Thurmond to serve for only one month. Normally, four new Thurmond selections would come to Washington to replace those pages who were leaving. The terrorist attacks earlier in the month caused a change in plans, though. No new Thurmond pages would be joining us, so we would have to say a sad goodbye to Vic, Arnold, Mary, and Amanda without the happy excitement of meeting their replacements.

This development was not surprising to all of us in Webster Hall. We were 16- and 17-year-old kids who understood just how scary and real the events of September 11th were. We were the first to understand why it wasn't possible to ask new kids to step into the confusion. None of us knew if the terrorist attacks were over or if they were only beginning, and it would have been irresponsible to bring more pages to Washington for one-month terms until the situation had stabilized. By the time these new pages had settled into their role and become comfortable with the circumstances of working in a terrorist target, their time would have ended.

The rest of us understood that we had already been battle-tested, and we performed well during that first month of service. With the confirmation that there would be no new Thurmond pages, it was clear that we would be the only individuals who could carry the torch for the U.S. Sen-

ate Page Program. If we gave up and went home, no new pages would be
sent to replace us—none of our young age, anyway. We had been told on
various occasions that college-aged men and women would do our jobs for
little or no pay, so it was possible that a stoppage in the current page program could lead to a very different program when and if it ever restarted.

The pressure was on us as juniors in high school to persevere because
it was clear that there were no replacements. The continuation of a program with origins dating back to 1829 would rest, at least in part, with
the determination of this group of pages. We had learned the lessons of
September 11th, though, and we felt that we were prepared to do what was
necessary.

Some workers in the Capitol described us as the best class, or one of
the best classes, of Senate pages ever. Many Senators and staff members
congratulated us on all our hard work and perseverance. Each of us would
accept these compliments graciously and modestly while understanding
that many of the incredible circumstances of our page experience were out
of our direct control. Each of us grew up quickly on September 11th, but it
is amazing to look back on the experience and realize that, through it all,
we were still just kids. We relied on one another to take life one day at a
time and keep everything in perspective.

We played practical jokes on each other. We made embarrassing mistakes while working on the Senate floor. We managed to find and create petty drama as well as any group of teenagers. We lived together and
worked together, and in the process we learned each other's quirks and
figured out how to push each other's buttons. We were one big, happy
family of brothers and sisters.

Some of my favorite stories to tell about my Senate page experience
concern the practical jokes that were played among the pages. The two
best pranks were pulled on the same poor page, Patrick Gibson. Patrick
was the most liberal page, but that wasn't the reason he was targeted for
these practical jokes. His roommates noticed that he had a hard time getting up on time in the morning. In fact, Patrick always cut it close to get to

school on time. For one of the practical jokes, some of the guys played on Patrick's fear that he would be late for school again.

One night the Senate remained in session until well past midnight. About half a dozen pages stayed late to finish up some last-minute work regarding a block of 120 or so amendments proposed by Senator Daniel Inouye (D-HI). I happened to be one of these pages who stayed late, and we didn't finish everything up until about 2:00 a.m. This was quite a story in itself, as it was the latest any of us had stayed in the Capitol, and it was pretty fun to run around the Capitol when it was so quiet. But the fun would really begin when we got back to Webster Hall shortly after 2:00 a.m.

Some of the Republican pages had arrived home a bit earlier. Two of them were Patrick's roommates, and when I got back, they were already plotting against Patrick, who was sleeping soundly. Those of us pages who had stayed late were still in our suits from work, so this gave one of Patrick's roommates an idea. We would pretend that it was morning and that we were ready to head down to school. We set Patrick's alarm clock forward to show him that he only had a couple minutes to get dressed.

After everyone was in on the plan, one of Patrick's roommates yelled, "Wake up, Patrick! You're going to be late for school!" What ensued was the fastest attempt to put on a suit and tie that I have ever witnessed. Patrick flailed around to get ready while the rest of us tried to contain our laughter. We even had one of our proctors in on this joke, so he unlocked the door in the basement to enter the school. Patrick ran down the stairs "to make it to school on time," only to find his roommates and the proctor laughing. He finally looked at the clock in the library and realized that it was 2:30 in the morning!

Two other factors made it all the more funny and amazing that the guys were able to pull this prank off. First, it happened to be 2:30 on a *Saturday* morning, so there was no school that day anyway! Second, we had been in session past 10:00 p.m. that night, which meant that we would not have had school the following day regardless of what day it was. Patrick had worked fairly late that night, though, so the guys executed a great prank by catching him at a confused and tired moment.

The other great prank was pulled in the Capitol Building itself. Most of the same culprits were involved, and Patrick was the target again because he had fallen asleep on a couch in the Senate lobby. It was something that happened to all of us for a few seconds at some time or another. The lobby was almost our break room. It was the place where we relaxed or did homework when it wasn't our turn to sit on the Senate floor or run errands. Patrick was out like a light on this occasion, though, so after a few minutes his roommate from Virginia, Clayton LaForge, decided to take advantage of the situation.

Clayton took Patrick's Senate ID, which is the size of any standard identification card, and enlarged it on the photocopier until it took up an entire 8.5x11-inch piece of paper. He then attached the piece of paper to Patrick's lanyard in place of the ID card. Now Patrick was sitting asleep in the Senate lobby with an enlarged photocopied picture of himself on his chest! This alone probably would have been funny enough to be memorable, but what happened next made it a classic.

No Senators had walked through the lobby during the time that Clayton was engineering this prank. Soon after the prank was completed, though, and all the other pages had been waved over to come take a look, Majority Leader Tom Daschle walked into the lobby on the same side where we were all standing. All of us simultaneously realized that this prank had just gotten a lot funnier, although we also worried that we might get into a lot of trouble for joking around in the lobby. Senator Daschle just glanced over at Patrick and announced to the rest of us, "There's an alert page!" The Senator seemed amused by the whole situation, and Clayton gave him a high-five! I still don't know what possessed Clayton to do that, but apparently the Senator found it as funny as we did.

In my four months serving as a page and sitting in that lobby, I think Senator Daschle walked to or from the Senate floor by that route maybe three times. The office of the majority leader is placed across the hall from a different entrance to the chamber, so he had no reason to come through the lobby. He did on that day, though, and it made for a classic moment for our class of Senate pages.

Patrick wasn't the only page who became the butt of our jokes. My roommate Jay and I would always pester our roommate Adam about his obsessive-compulsive nature, especially in regard to alarm clocks. Adam was very nervous about making sure that we woke up on time and made it to school on time. He insisted that all of our alarm clocks were set, and set correctly, before we went to bed each night. Jay and I would sometimes give Adam a hard time by casually bluffing as we got into bed that we weren't going to set our alarm clock that night. Adam would flip out on us, and we would just laugh because that was exactly the reaction we were looking for.

One night we were especially hounding Adam on the issue. We pretended we were worried about the way Adam had set his alarm clock, and we asked him if he was sure it was set for the right time. He double-checked it, then got into his top bunk above Jay. Jay asked if Adam had really double-checked it. Adam answered that he had, but we could tell that he was already nervous about it again. We kept asking him about it until he got all the way down from his bed and triple-checked it!

My friends Scott Moore and Kevin Burleson also provided plenty of memorable moments. They were roommates and became good friends quickly. They were definitely two of the smartest pages in my class, but they also knew how to have fun (and get into some mild trouble in the process). Scott and Kevin loved to play Frisbee; they even made up business cards to that effect. They called their organization Senate Page Frisbee or SPF. Their names were listed on the business card, along with one of their slogans, "We answer only to God." Well, apparently they also answered to the Capitol Police, because one day they got into trouble for playing on the Capitol grounds. They also managed to get scolded for playing Frisbee on our field trips to Fort McHenry and Mount Vernon!

We pages also developed our own inside jokes to keep the mood light. Kevin and I loved to watch the movie *Office Space*, which comically depicts the monotonous life of a cubicle worker in a big company. We often used references or direct quotes from the movie at work in the Capitol when we had to do something boring or annoying. It spoke to the fact that we understood we were growing up fast, but we wanted to stay kids and have as much fun as we could before any "real jobs" came our way.

Several other funny incidents occurred while we were working on the Senate floor. Every day was a new day for the pages, and while our jobs were largely the same from day to day, we had no idea what individual tasks might be asked of us next. Predictably, we all made plenty of little mistakes. We knew that C-SPAN2 was capturing all of our actions while we were on the Senate floor, so some mishaps were especially embarrassing. I remember one page tripping a bit while walking up the stairs to retrieve a newly proposed amendment from a Senator. She was so embarrassed that she sat in the lobby the rest of the day! I also remember water being spilled on a Senator's desk, and a full glass of water being dropped and shattered just outside the Senate Chamber.

My own embarrassing moments include walking all the way over to the Russell Senate Office Building, only to forget which room I needed to go to. I had to go all the way back to the Democratic cloakroom and ask where I was going again! Considering all the trips we made, though, this one mistake still made for a pretty good success percentage!

Another time I was given a message for Senator Evan Bayh (D-IN). I was told to get it to him right away. When I walked back out to the Senate floor, Bayh was nowhere to be seen. I asked the other pages if anyone had seen him lately. I took the folded piece of paper with Bayh's name on it, set it down near the rostrum and began waiting for the Senator to arrive. What I didn't know was that the location of the Senator was on the inside of the note along with the message! All the pages are taught not to read the written messages given to us, though, so I had no way of knowing. Eventually, I took the message back into the cloakroom, and told the staff that Senator Bayh had not come to the floor yet. They laughed a little when they figured out the communication mistake, and I eventually got Bayh his message!

The most intense mishap on the Senate floor occurred one morning as all the pages set up the chamber for the day's session. Katie Ruedebusch, one of my fellow pages from South Dakota, was walking around the Senate chamber making sure each desk had the appropriate documents on it. Each of the desks is a priceless historical object, many dating back at least to the Civil War. Throughout the nation's history, as new states joined the union, two new desks were made as exact replicas. As Katie walked by Senator Schumer's desk, she brushed up against it and knocked a piece of the top part of the desk off! Luckily, only a small piece of wood had come off, and it was fixed in a couple of days. She had barely brushed by the back part of the desk, so the piece must have been loose or cracked already. It made for a crazy situation for the pages that morning, but I sincerely doubt Schumer ever even noticed. Now, we can all laugh about it and tease Katie for breaking Schumer's desk, but at the time she took it pretty hard.

A telling of all the crazy moments and antics of my Senate page class would not be complete without an account of the boy/girl drama we all had from time to time. It all started innocently enough (as it always does) with a desire to meet some of the U.S. House pages and hear their stories from September 11th. Some of the male Senate pages learned the location of the residence of the House pages in the week after the terrorist attacks, and we decided to make a visit.

I tagged along with about a half dozen of the guys to go meet some of our rival pages. When we arrived at their residence, we made a few new friends and asked about what things had been like for them on 9/11. After talking for a while, we invited anyone who wanted to join us to go to Union Station for dinner. A handful of female House pages took us up on our offer, but none of the guys did. After dinner at Union Station, we asked if any of the girls wanted to see our beloved Webster Hall. And thus was made the biggest mistake of our journey to meet some House pages.

The girls back at Webster took offense to our bringing other girls over. The situation ended up being very awkward, as you could cut the tension and jealousy in the air with a knife. After the House pages left, the Senate girls quickly rallied together and gave us a piece of their collective mind.

They thought we were trying to replace them with new friends. They even had a bedtime pow-wow on their floor that night dedicated to bashing us and the House pages we had invited to Webster. Oh, the drama!

It took a few days, but emotions were settled. We assured the Senate girls that they could not be replaced, and we didn't see much of the House pages after that anyway. It was my first experience with the all-powerful glare that women can give when a man has done something the least bit objectionable. In the end, it could be one of the more important lessons I learned while living in the social context of Webster Hall!

Looking back on all the drama that occurred among the pages, the vast majority of it was petty differences and misunderstandings, which is reassuring in a way. It means that we were normal teenagers. The lessons learned were that, even on Capitol Hill, kids will be kids, and you can't change human nature. I would have thought that there was already more than enough excitement and drama going on during the months that we were Senate pages, but a group of teenagers in an enclosed space will always find a way to create some more.

Luckily, all the drama from the House page fiasco had cleared up by the time the four Thurmond pages had to leave us. We would all miss each one of them because they had shared a common experience with us in a trying time. Jay, Adam, and I had become good friends with our fourth roommate, Vic, so we would miss him especially. Our room would be down to only three pages now, and there would be no replacement sent from South Carolina.

On his way out of the room, Vic signed the inside of his desk drawer, as many previous pages had done, with his name and home state. He also wrote a poignant note that would symbolize a major part of our Senate page class's experience, "I survived September 11, 2001." Adam, Jay, and I would now have to move forward without Vic and keep on surviving and serving our U.S. Senate. There would be more hardships to come, and it was hard to have four of our newest friends go home. Yet we felt battle-tested and purpose-driven, and we were having the most fun of our lives.

CHAPTER 11
R.I.P. THURMOND
AND WELLSTONE

S enator Harry Reid abruptly called for a recess from his front row desk on October 2, 2001. I was sitting on the rostrum steps listening to Senator Tom Carper (D-DE) at the time, and the other pages and I were somewhat taken aback at the seemingly rude interruption of Carper, who began to object to the sudden call for the recess.

The presiding officer could not bring the Senate to recess until a vote was taken on the matter or Carper rescinded his objection. Unbeknownst to Senator Carper and the Democratic pages, Senator Strom Thurmond had just collapsed at his desk. Both Reid and a high-level Democratic staff member yelled at Carper to withdraw his objection. Carper then realized that there was a medical emergency on the floor of the U.S. Senate and withdrew his objection.

We stood up from the rostrum to see what was happening on the other side of the aisle. Senator Bill Frist, a medical doctor, happened to be in the chamber and was attending to the 98-year-old Thurmond. By the time I realized that it was Thurmond who was down on the ground, the Senate was whirling with action.

The presiding officer snapped the gavel, officially putting the Senate into recess, which would then stop the live C-SPAN2 coverage of this event. The majority leader burst through the doors from the Democratic side of the chamber, and EMTs came in with a stretcher for Thurmond. The galleries were cleared, and all staff members were asked to leave the Senate chamber as well.

All of the Democratic pages retreated to the lobby, where we joined our friends from the Republican side. One Republican page who had witnessed the collapse was visibly upset, and that got me somewhat worried. Had we all just witnessed the death of Strom Thurmond? It was a thought that was never too far from our minds. A handful of the Senators were well into their 70s or 80s, but Thurmond was nearly 99 years old. It would not have been all that unexpected if Thurmond had died while still in office.

As these thoughts passed through my mind, someone herded all the pages further from the chamber. We went out the Democratic end of the lobby and entered the President's Room. This is a ceremonial room for the President of the United States. For example, President Lyndon Johnson signed the Voting Rights Act of 1965 in this room. In recent years, Presidents have used it more rarely, while Senators have used it fairly frequently for press conferences and interviews. On this day, it served the function of a hospital waiting room for all the Senate pages waiting for the news about one of our 100 bosses.

Some others tried to console one of the pages who had started crying. All of the other Republican pages who had been sitting on the rostrum directly in front of Thurmond were explaining what they had seen. My roommate Adam Anthony had just set a glass of water on Thurmond's desk and sat back down to the rostrum. Adam told me that he had seen Thurmond begin to fall out of his chair as if he were fainting. He explained that Thurmond's staff member had helped Thurmond to lie on the ground, and Senator Frist had responded quickly by rushing to Thurmond's side.

Soon after Adam explained the play-by-play of what had occurred on the other side of the rostrum, we received some good news. Thurmond was conscious and speaking. Still, the EMTs took him out on the stretcher and examined him. Later on we learned that he had fainted from dehydration. Of course, this led to endless teasing of Adam regarding his duties as a page to bring the Senator his water! Although he wasn't at fault in any way, Adam actually did feel a little guilty about the ordeal. Luckily, Thurmond turned out to be fine, and we would just chalk it up as yet another crazy day for the fall 2001 class of Senate pages.

Especially after this scary day with Senator Thurmond, every trip to the sergeant at arms's office offered the pages a morbid reminder of the possibility of the death of sitting U.S. Senator. Two pages would go to the sergeant at arms's office before the start of each day's session to pick up the presiding officer's gavel and upon the adjournment of each day's session to return the gavel. While I was a page, a black piece of fabric was kept in the same place as the gavel. This black cloth would be draped over a Senator's desk in the event of his or her death.

With the likes of Senators Jesse Helms (R-NC), Robert Byrd, and Strom Thurmond, a death by natural causes of old age was a real possibility, but now we also lived in an age of terror in which the Capitol Building and our leadership were targets. Each time I had the honor of making this ceremonial trip to retrieve the gavel, the black cloth would serve as yet another reminder of the value of life and the possibilities for death. Both the Senate and the House leadership were assigned Capitol Police security details, and the Capitol Building itself was under heightened security.

My class of Senate pages was fortunate enough to avoid the devastating mental blow of losing a Senator to death by any cause. We felt a sense of loyalty to all 100 of our bosses in the 107th Congress. We built up our own confidence by watching these men and women carry themselves with such strength in troubled times. Losing a Senator on either side of the aisle, even if only to natural causes, would have been another difficult challenge for us to conquer.

Two Senators from the 107th Congress have passed on since I left Washington in January of 2002. Senator Paul Wellstone died on October 25, 2002, in a plane crash, and recently retired Senator Thurmond died June 26, 2003, at the age of 100. The two men make for a remarkable comparison on many levels.

The most important difference as far as the functioning of the U.S. Senate was concerned was the drastically different circumstances in their respective deaths. Paul Wellstone died only a couple of weeks before what would most likely have been his reelection, as Wellstone led in the polls over challenger Norm Coleman. What followed were sad days in the U.S. Senate. The black cloth that I mentioned was placed over Wellstone's desk in the Senate chamber.

I remember hearing the news of the crash while back home in South Dakota. I was in school at the time I heard the news, but as soon as I got home I called a great friend of mine from my Senate page days. Jen Holden had been sponsored by Senator Wellstone, and like me, she was a Republican "trapped" inside a Democratic Page appointment. Her Senator was one of the most liberal members of the Senate, and my Senator was the leader of the Democratic Party. One could probably see how we bonded!

While talking to her on the phone, though, I could tell that she was devastated and shocked. She had formed a personal connection with Wellstone that had no regard for party politics. Jen remembered Wellstone as the Senator who made an incredible experience possible. That was the consensus among all of the other pages I would speak with in the wake of the Wellstone tragedy. The universal sentiment spoke to the commitment we all had to the Senate as the greatest legislative body in the world and to our 100 bosses.

All my Senate page friends felt the pain of losing such an impassioned member of the Senate. My memories of Wellstone mainly include his heartfelt speeches on the Senate floor. I would find myself disagreeing with what he had to say while simultaneously admiring him. The space immediately around his desk could never contain him. He would pace actively while addressing the Senate. His desk was on an aisle dividing the Democratic desks, and he would often spend more time standing in that aisle than behind his desk. He would stretch the microphone attached to his desk as far as it would allow, and he would plead with his fellow Senators to see the issue his way.

He was impassioned, but, apparently, not particularly convincing. Whenever there was a 99-1 vote during Wellstone's time as a Senator, it would be a decent bet that Wellstone was the one. It was a form of political courage mixed with a liberal eccentricity that led the Minnesotan to take stands for the sake of taking them.

Although I am sure I heard him speak on the floor countless times, as he frequented the chamber often, I only specifically remember listening to Wellstone speak on one topic. As the war in Afghanistan began, Wellstone led a cause for more food aid and medical supplies to the Afghan people. He explained that the warlords were rounding up what had been airlifted in so far, and the people who needed it were not necessarily getting it. He called for a massive increase in these forms of direct aid to the Afghan people, and I credit him for the spirit he brought to the floor on that issue.

I tried to think specifically what Wellstone might be saying about the current status of the War on Terror. Most likely he would be championing the cause of alleged U.S. torture tactics and watching for any bad apples in the U.S. military to be indicators of a broader policy of torture by Secretary Rumsfeld. Although this assessment is probably accurate, I would like to think that Wellstone would also be capable of coming to the Senate floor to comment on the amazing liberation of those in Afghanistan.

He had just enough of an independent streak in him that I could see him taking a day off from Bush bashing to note the incredible strides made in the social world of the average Afghan woman. I can imagine him pacing behind his desk recounting the atrocities that the Taliban placed on the entire population, and especially women. I can see him stepping out from behind his desk, with nothing between him and the pages sitting on the rostrum steps, and speaking with his amazing compassion for the poor. I hope Wellstone would have taken up that attitude and congratulated President Bush and America on freeing the people of Afghanistan and introducing an entire country to basic civil rights.

Unfortunately, we will never know exactly what Wellstone would have to say because of his tragic death. Another unfortunate event followed the Senator's death in the form of his own remembrance ceremony. Many argued that the speeches went overboard, and the event turned into more of a partisan political rally than a celebration of Paul Wellstone's life. It was even reported that Senator Trent Lott was booed by some in the large crowd. Who gets booed at an event that amounts to a funeral? Well, apparently the former Republican leader does because of the partisan charge electrifying the crowd. All of this helped lead to the eventual victory of Norm Coleman over Walter Mondale, who had replaced Wellstone as the Democratic candidate.

Senator Thurmond's death did not have the direct impact on the Senate that Wellstone's death did. Wellstone was replaced temporarily by Minnesota Governor Jesse Ventura's appointment of Independent Dean Barkley, and then eventually succeeded by Coleman. Thurmond, on the other hand, had been retired from the Senate for over a year when he passed away, and Senator Lindsey Graham had been elected to replace Thurmond.

While Wellstone's death caused enough of a stir for the GOP to pick up a seat, we all remember how Thurmond's retirement indirectly caused a major political shake-up of its own. Senator Lott received much more than booing after comments he made at a party celebrating Thurmond's 100th birthday and retirement from the Senate; he received a pink slip for the position of Republican leader. Although I would argue that his comments were of little harm when put into context, the political winds blew hard enough that Lott's enemies within the GOP saw their chance to mow over the Mississippi Senator.

When Lott said that he was proud of his state's support for Thurmond's presidential bid in 1948, he did so in a run-of-the-mill pandering way that plenty of politicians use all the time. Lott wanted to puff up the retiring Senator with the flattering comment that Lott's own home state had always thought highly of Thurmond. The reference to Thurmond's presidential bid, which was largely based on support for segregation, was clearly a poor choice. Lott went on to say that the country might be better off today if more states had followed Mississippi's lead and had voted for Thurmond.

When watching the tape of Lott's comments, it is fairly easy to see the gears in his head turning hard to compliment both his home state and Thurmond at the same time in some grandiose way. The real lesson learned from Lott's incident is that a politician should not try to compliment a Senator with a segregationist past by just winging it. To his credit, Lott did apologize for the possibility of offense to be found in his unprepared comments for Thurmond. In the end, though, Lott was guilty of little more than awkward flattery.

While I remember the specific contents of only one Wellstone speech, I remember witnessing only one speech given by Senator Thurmond while I was a page. It came on his 99th birthday in December of 2001. Both Senators Daschle and Lott had come to the floor to congratulate Thurmond on his years of service and to wish him a happy birthday. One of the Senators invited a round of applause in the Senate chamber for Thurmond, so all the Senate pages stood and clapped.

We remained standing and waited for Thurmond to respond. He stood up at his desk with the help of a staff member and proceeded to thank the other Senators for their kind words. He scanned the whole chamber and said words that I will never forget, "I love you all. Especially, you ladies. You are beautiful!" He then sat back down, and the Senate carried on with the rest of its business for the day.

All of the pages chuckled at Thurmond's words. It would have been funny even as an isolated event, but his little speech was consistent with a bunch of other quirky behaviors that defined him to the pages. Adam told me that Thurmond made a similar speech at a weekly Republican caucus luncheon. Thurmond concluded his thoughts with a look around the room and another line to the effect of, "I love all you ladies. All you ladies are beautiful!"

My roommate Jay had the greatest Strom Thurmond story from being a page on the Republican side. One day Thurmond called Jay over and reached into his desk for a piece of candy. Many of the Republican pages had been called up at various times to get a piece of candy from Thurmond, and the Senator would often instruct the page to give it to another person, usually a female staff member. Jay had a unique situation on his hands, though. Thurmond gave Jay the piece of candy and pointed across the chamber to Senator Hillary Clinton! Jay had to walk across the chamber and interrupt Senator Clinton's work so she could receive a piece of candy. And then, like a middle-man in an elementary school crush, he had to explain that the candy was from Senator Thurmond!

Another Thurmond story shows the effect of the Senator's age on his ability to do his job. Virtually the only time Thurmond came to the Senate floor was for roll call votes. On his way into the chamber, a staff member would have to explain to him which way he would be voting. I am guessing that Thurmond did not know exactly what he was voting for or against on many occasions, but that argument could probably be used against many other Senators who could not use age as an excuse for not keeping up with every vote.

One funny instance of Thurmond's reflexive voting at the prompting of his staff came the day after September 11th. All of the Senators had gathered for a vote on the resolution condemning the terrorist attacks. The clerk was calling the roll alphabetically, and he got to Senator Fred Thompson (R-TN) who came right before Thurmond on the list. Either he heard incorrectly or his staff signaled him to vote too early, but Thurmond bellowed "Aye" immediately after the clerk called for Thompson's vote. The clerk went on without trouble, though, attributing the vote to Thurmond and then returning to Thompson to get his vote.

Thurmond and Wellstone would reply with the same "Aye" on this vote, but one would be hard-pressed to find a more different pair of U.S. Senators from the 107th Congress. Thurmond and Wellstone are the only two at the time of this writing to have passed on from the set of Senators I served. Thurmond was arguably the most conservative, and Wellstone was probably the most liberal. Wellstone had an amazing amount of fire and passion for making speeches, while Thurmond was too old to do much more than enter the chamber for a vote. The circumstances of their deaths were also vastly different, as Thurmond's was essentially expected while Wellstone's caught us all off guard.

The reaction to their deaths from my fellow pages was similar, though. We all understood the historic time during which we were able to serve the

U.S. Senate, and we all understood that a piece of that legislative body was lost
with the passing of each man. I can only hope that these two men are looking
down on the U.S. Senate and still consider it to be the greatest legislative body
in the world.

CHAPTER 12
ANTHRAX

A month after the September 11th attacks, it was all too clear what four airliners loaded with jet fuel could do to a country. On October 15, 2001, America learned what a small amount of powder in an envelope could do. A letter laced with anthrax was opened in Senator Daschle's office in the Hart Building, a building the Senate pages walked through every day on the way to the Capitol. Most pages would run at least one errand each day to the Hart Building.

I went to the Hart Building and Senator Daschle's office even more frequently than the average page. There was never a shortage of errands to run to Daschle's office, and in the early days of my time as a page, many of these errands would be given to me or to one of the other two pages from South Dakota, since everyone assumed that Katie, Jason, and I knew where our Senator's office was located. Even after the first couple of weeks, I would jump at the chance to make the trip over to the Hart Building and deliver messages for my home-state Senator.

On the morning of October 15, a staff member in Senator Daschle's office opened a letter with a seemingly innocent return address of an elementary school in New Jersey. The suspicious powder that came out of the envelope was identified as anthrax. The writer of the note inside the envelope referenced 9/11 and presented himself as a Muslim extremist with a weak grasp of English syntax and intentions of harming both Israel and America. Some speculate that the perpetrators were not part of al-

Qaeda but were opportunistically taking advantage of the recent al-Qaeda attacks to provide cover for their own anthrax plot. The effects of the anthrax were not limited to Senator Daschle's office. For example, a similar letter was sent to NBC broadcaster Tom Brokaw at his office in New York City. Another sad consequence was the deaths of innocent postal workers who handled the letters on their way to their targets. To this day no one has been charged with the anthrax attacks through the mail system along the East Coast.

These attacks resulted in the deaths of five Americans and caused much discomfort with the mail service. Citizens throughout the U.S. were worried about opening their mail or worried that their mail had come into contact with other contaminated mail. Not surprisingly, Washington, D.C., and the Capitol mail system cracked down on this problem immediately to decontaminate the mail and get it moving again. From that point on, all mail was irradiated and a corner of each envelope was clipped so any powder could fall out. It was kind of funny to see the envelopes I received in the mail with a cut corner and a yellow tinge from irradiation, as if my mom might be sending me some anthrax, but at the same time it was a bitter reminder of the new reality in Washington, D.C.

In the days after the opening of the anthrax letter, Senator Daschle would often come to the Senate chamber to address his colleagues and the nation regarding the anthrax attack on his office. Daschle would walk across the hall from his majority leader office and enter the chamber. Upon seeing him approach, the page on point would quickly get him a glass of water for his desk. Daschle would be recognized by the presiding officer immediately, and we would all hang on the Senator's every word in the hope of any good news. He would update the public on the status of the investigation and the clean-up process in a matter-of-fact tone.

His real purpose for addressing the public came through as he spoke of his staff members. He still spoke in a soft, smooth voice, but he conveyed a certain level of emotion. It was clear that his top priority was taking care of his people, which is what we should expect from all of our leaders. Daschle delivered news on how many members of his staff had inhaled anthrax spores and on how they were feeling. As the days passed by, the outlook seemed bright, as medication had been given to the staff quickly enough to save their lives. Still, the good news was in itself a reminder of how bad the situation could have been and how severe the threat was.

By mid-October security in and around the Capitol was heightened to an interesting degree. The Capitol Building was clearly a high value target for any terrorist, so it was a scary place to work day in and day out. At the same time, the level of security and the professionalism of the Capitol Police made its grounds the safest place in Washington, with the exception of the White House. This safety paradox was tossed around a lot as we all carried a certain level of anxiety about working in a terrorist target, but we were often reassured by the Capitol Police and others that we were "in the safest place possible."

Surely, the Capitol was much safer from a truck bomb because of the vigilant officers and the concrete barriers. The problem in October was that the Capitol Police and concrete barriers aren't in the business of stopping powder in the mail. This was a new form of warfare that had intense consequences. The threat facing our nation was now known to be much more subtle and malleable than plans involving big explosions and hijacked aircraft. We would have no choice, though, but to adjust and continue the work of the legislative branch.

The Hart Building was closed down for full decontamination days after the Daschle letter was opened. It was worried that the tiny anthrax spores may have entered the ventilation system and spread throughout the building. One of the objectives of those charged with securing the Capitol complex was to determine how far the spores may have traveled. One way to determine this was to test all the Capitol workers for inhalation anthrax by means of a nasal swab test. Of course, the Senate pages were included in this group, so we all had to get in line on October 17 and receive a surprisingly deep shove into our nostrils.

The day before, some of us had gathered around Senator Frist in the lobby. We all knew his background as a medical doctor, so we trusted his opinion. He was very decisive in what he had to say to us. After explaining the basics of what anthrax was, he told us that we had a "zero percent" chance of being infected. The process of testing all the Capitol workers was seen more as a tool to confirm that the anthrax had not spread past Daschle's office.

Frist's assurances made us feel more comfortable about the situation, but the nasal swab was anything but comfortable. One page even fainted for a moment after the deep penetration of the nasal swab. When I tried to relay this news to other pages, I got a lesson in the difficulty of public relations in such a nervous atmosphere. I told a couple of girls that this page "had some kind of reaction to the test," and before I could say anything more, they started freaking out. They took those words to mean that he had tested positive for anthrax spores in his nose. I quickly tried to further my explanation, "No! No! He's fine. He fainted or passed out when they stuck the swab up his nose! They don't have any results of the tests back. He passed out for a couple seconds because of the swab."

The girls fumed and scolded me for not being careful in my choice of words. After the fact, I realized that they were right, but it goes to show how difficult it is to relay information with anxiety running high. We would all be informed that our tests were negative a few days later. In the meantime, we were all placed on an antibiotic called Ciprofloxacin as a precautionary measure. We were given a six-day supply, but once our results came back negative, we were told we could stop using the drug.

One notable exception to this order was my friend Jen Cohen. She was on a sixty-day supply of Cipro, as were Daschle's staffers and the Capitol Police officers that had entered the Hart office that day. Jen was my head page, so her duties usually limited her to keeping things organized on the Senate floor. On the morning of October 15, though, a cloakroom staff member had given her a delivery for Daschle's office in the Hart Building. The session hadn't started yet that morning, so Jen was free to run errands. It was a relatively rare opportunity for her to get out and about, so she took up the task happily. It was a simple errand that I had done dozens of times, and I would have had a good chance of doing that very one if Jen hadn't been standing right there in the cloakroom at that moment.

Jen actually entered Daschle's office and delivered the information before the anthrax letter had even been opened. She spent ten seconds in the office at most, but this was enough to place her on a heightened medical status. This meant that she would be taking medicine for a couple of months instead of a handful of days. Even though her test came back negative, like those of all the other pages, she would stay on the medication as a precaution. On the face of it, the extended regimen shouldn't have been a big deal, but Jen suffered nagging side effects with the medication that wore her down to exhaustion. On top of all the other stress we were under, headaches, sore throats, and a loss of appetite haunted Jen.

It was heartbreaking for me to watch Jen in such pain day after day. Jen and I had become great friends while we were Senate pages. Our bond began when we learned that we shared the same birthday. We made it through September 11th together, as well as the evacuation that occurred on our joint 17th birthday two days later. I enjoyed working with Jen on the Senate floor, and she made a great head page. We shared many happy and fun moments together during a time period plagued with grief and fear.

After the anthrax attack, Jen became my closest friend in the page program. I look back now and realize that she was the first person outside my own family that I truly loved, in the sense that love is defined as a condition in which your own happiness depends on the happiness of another. When Jen was in agonizing pain from the side effects of her medication, she cried that she wanted to go home. I recall moments when I felt afraid, anxious, and homesick while I served as a Senate page, but the only instances when I remember being truly unhappy were those days when Jen was unhappy. All of the pages sympathized with her because we knew it could have been any one of us who had run that errand to Daschle's office. Jen had amazing perseverance, though, and she made it through the program, missing only a few days of work due to illness despite the challenges placed upon her.

Some of my happiest days as a page were those days when Jen was doing well. She had the most beautiful smile I had ever seen, and her enthusiasm was contagious. I remember getting home from a late night of work on a day when Jen had left early. She was waiting for me with a big hug and an even bigger smile, two good signs that she was feeling better. As Jen and I spent most of our free time together, some of the guys started to tease me that she must be my girlfriend. One female page even made the comment one day that Jen and I "made a cute couple." As much as I enjoyed being placed in the same league as this beautiful girl by my fellow pages, our relationship never reached a romantic level. I learned a lot about love, though, because I learned how to care about someone else's well-being more than my own. I know now that I was too young to understand and appreciate romantic love anyway, but I thank God for the great lesson in love and friendship.

Putting others ahead of oneself was a key principle that all the pages grew to understand more each day. We honored the heroes of September 11th from a personal perspective. We relied on the service of the Capitol Police for our protection. We witnessed the dedication of the Senators and their staff members. All of these examples of service stuck with me, but the service of my fellow Senate pages was especially important to me. Each page looked out for all the others as we became a family forged in these tumultuous times. It gave me great comfort to know that all the pages were there for me no matter what other circumstances would be thrown at us. The least I could do was to be there for them as well.

Jen let me be there for her, and she rewarded me with an invitation to another celebration of family—a home-cooked meal. Jen's father was a close friend of Senator Kent Conrad of North Dakota. Through this connection, Jen's family had also become friends with some of Conrad's staff, especially a senior staffer named Geri. After learning of the unfortunate situation Jen was in on the day of the anthrax attack, Geri invited Jen over to her home for dinner. Jen brought me along, and it was a great experience for both of us. Jen needed the comfort of a good family friend, and I sure didn't mind the North Dakota hospitality.

It was three days after the anthrax letter was opened that we shared a great meal with Geri and her husband, George. The meal of meat and potatoes was a great reminder of home, and the North Dakota accents were fun as well! As Jen and Geri set the table before the delicious meal, I spoke in the living room with George. After making small talk for a while and sharing our experiences from the craziness of September 11th and the anthrax attack, he turned the conversation deadly serious for a moment. He shared with me some no-nonsense advice about the reality of living in Washington, D.C., and working in the Capitol complex. It was clear that he worried about his wife and also sincerely cared for Jen and me. His advice was blunt and to the point when he said, "Just run!" This was the advice he had for responding to a terrorist attack that might befall the Capitol any day now in a post-9/11 world.

I nodded solemnly and promised that I would do as he said. Of course, by this time in the page program I knew that while this advice was well intended and mostly correct, there was an important corollary. I looked over and caught a glance of Jen in the dining room and realized that the important addition to his advice was the word "together." All the pages had made it to this point together, and the Army Ranger philosophy of "leave no man behind" was plain in my mind. There was no cowardice, only intelligence, in fleeing the Capitol as quickly as possible in the event of a bombing or shooting attack. At the same time, it was an ingrained part of our character and experience as Senate pages to help each other through any future hardship. We had the Senators for leadership and the Capitol Police for protection, but if worse came to worst, we would "just run *together*."

By mid-October all the pages held to this philosophy. That made it all the more difficult to deal with one page's exit from the program. Christina Valentine lived in northern Virginia, and her parents pulled her out of the program shortly after the anthrax attacks. I always saw it as a situation where her parents felt Christina was so close, yet so far away. Living in northern Virginia, they could come to visit their daughter at any time, so they had a certain level of control over their daughter's page experience. In August of 2001, sending her to school in Washington must have seemed like an easy thing to do for one semester. The reality of the terrorist threat changed that calculation, though, and they made a completely rational decision to bring Christina home.

After the discovery of anthrax in the Hart Building, all of the pages were counseled that it was up to us to decide whether or not to exit the program. No one would be looked down upon for wanting to leave. All of the pages had conversations with their parents on the topic. Rumors swirled that all of the pages would be sent home, regardless of our wishes, because of the liability risks. With thirty sets of worried parents, two terrorist incidents behind us, and plenty of unknowns going into the future, it seemed to be not a matter of if we would lose pages from the program, but when and how many. We were lucky that the program survived and only one set of parents pulled their child.

In my recent conversations with Christina, she has recounted some of her feelings from this trying time in her life. Christina made it clear to me, as she had to all the pages back in 2001, that she sincerely wanted to stay and see it though until January with the rest of us. She felt a strong bond with her new friends and roommates in Webster Hall, and she loved working for the U.S. Senate. Her parents made a different decision, though, and they were the ones with the authority to make that decision for their daughter. I was very proud of Christina's effort to make the best out of a difficult situation.

Christina and her family invited all the pages over for a Sunday dinner a few weeks after she went home. Sunday dinners were a staple of life in Webster Hall. The proctors tried to get a new ethnic food for us each week. We would have a weekly meeting at which the proctors would make any necessary announcements, and then we would eat some Indian, Thai, or Japanese food. It was fun to try new types of food each week, but we all looked forward to this special chance to see Christina again and meet her family.

Christina cooked the meal herself and was a great hostess. We all had a great time, and it was a good change of pace for our Sunday dinner line-up. It was clear that Christina was still a part of our group despite being technically out of the page program. She assured us that she would come to the closing ceremony in January and would keep in touch.

While the delicious meals made by Geri and Christina provided a good diversion from the heavy thoughts of the day, the issue of anthrax did not fade away. The Hart Building was closed, which meant that a significant number of Senators' offices were displaced. Temporary offices were set up in the basement of the Capitol and in spare space in the Russell and Dirksen Buildings. This made our jobs as pages all the more difficult, as we had to navigate new intricacies in the Capitol complex and communicate with each Senator's staff as they moved into new space.

The Hart Building would be closed for the entire remainder of our term as pages. We would be forced to walk another block down the road to the Dirksen Building in the cold months of winter to enter the Capitol complex. Of course, this was only a mild inconvenience compared to the other issues that loomed large in our minds. Some reports at the time warned of more terrorist attacks in the areas that had experienced anthrax letters. New York, Washington, and Florida police were stretched thin with the anthrax issues, so these locations may have been a weak point for terrorists to exploit.

Another anthrax letter addressed to Senator Patrick Leahy (D-VT) was soon discovered, and the power of such biological weapons was proved. Fear plagued the mail system, and many government buildings other than the Hart Building were searched for signs of anthrax. We were even booted from Webster Hall for an afternoon while men in moon suits searched for traces of the substance.

The other great fear coming to the surface was the dreaded smallpox. The disease had essentially been wiped off the planet through a successful vaccination campaign. One fear was that a terrorist could give himself the disease and make a visit to the Capitol Building, spreading the disease to innocent civilians and possibly our nation's leaders. There is truly no telling what a suicidal group of Islamic extremists is capable of attempting or accomplishing. As the risks of terrorist events like biological warfare became more realistic, more credence was given to the idea of moving the business of Congress to a more secure location like a military base.

Under this scenario I heard of two different fates of the Senate page program. First, and more likely, we would simply be eliminated and sent home. The other option was favored by one of our proctors, who said that the pages would be taken along as "necessary to the business of the Senate." While it was hard to imagine the Senate conducting business on a military base, it might have only been one more terrorist action away. The idea of our legislative branch is synonymous with openness and freedom, so retreating to a military base would have been an option of last resort. It was even harder to imagine myself and my fellow pages continuing to do our jobs in any environment other than the U.S. Capitol Building.

Another intense rumor made the rounds among the pages in the aftermath of the anthrax situation. We all talked about the possibility that we might be asked to stay on for another semester. The Senate page program was a one-semester program, but we understood that it might be difficult for the program to ask new teenagers to enter into a dangerous setting. We knew that no new pages had come to replace the Thurmond pages at the end of October, so the question intensified after the discovery of anthrax: would any new pages come to replace us? All of us had grown up a lot in our first two months in Washington. We had grown to understand that the end of the page program as we knew it was a possibility. Most of the other pages I talked to about this possibility said they would stay on if asked. We were growing weary from the long days and the unusual challenges during our term as pages, but we understood the importance of the page program and of our service to the U.S. Senate. If we had been asked to stay on for another semester, I am confident that many of us would have "reenlisted" in an effort to maintain the page program for the future and fight the War on Terror in our own symbolic way.

Luckily, the anthrax discovered in Daschle's office on October 15, 2001, was the last threat to our well-being during our term as pages. The worries over more anthrax or worse, smallpox, never came to fruition. The situation stabilized enough for a fresh group of high school juniors to come in as our replacements in January. This is the beauty of hindsight, though. My group of pages still had a long road to travel to mid-January without the beneficial knowledge that the attacks had concluded. Clearly, September and October had been the longest and most difficult months of my life, but there was still much to learn and accomplish through November, December, and January.

CHAPTER 13
POP CULTURE

E ven after the attacks on our homeland, popular culture per-
sisted in America. Americans could escape the bitter realities of our new post-9/11 world by taking in the fun of sports,
music, and television. Everyone needed a break from the 24-hour cable
news updates once in a while to take in some of the baseball playoffs or
relax to some music. The Senate pages were no different. We tried to find
some time on nights when the homework load wasn't too heavy to unwind
with some fun entertainment.

The mood toward the popular culture of the day had shifted slightly,
though. Now the New York Yankees were America's team, and the heroes
of the World Series were inspiring figures second only to the real heroes
working hard at Ground Zero. Lyrics of songs became more powerful than
their authors could have known. Television programs found themselves
with the dual role of entertaining and educating. Popular culture and the
American public endured the terrorist attacks together. In a country of
political apathy where many citizens can't identify cabinet-level officials
or leaders of Congress, professional athletes and artists provide much-
needed inspiration where politicians sometimes fail.

In 2001, the October Classic ran into November, and what a classic it
was! The Arizona Diamondbacks hosted the New York Yankees in Game 7
of the World Series. I don't remember catching much of the other games
leading up to Game 7, but many of the other pages and I sat down to watch

the game that would decide the series. Most of us had mixed feelings about who to root for, because the Yankees had truly become America's team in the weeks since September 11th, but they were the defending champs with a huge budget. The Diamondbacks were a relatively new team to the league, and fans had compelling reasons to root for them as the obvious underdogs taking on the Yankee dynasty. A couple of pages from the New England area cheered for the Yankees outright, and the rest of us cheered for a close game. America deserved a great baseball game, and it was delivered all the way through the bottom of the ninth.

The Diamondbacks took on the role of underdogs as they came to bat down one run in the last half of the ninth inning. The game soon provided a childhood backyard baseball moment for Arizona's Luis Gonzalez, whose teammate, Tony Womack, had driven in the tying run. The bases were loaded with only one out, and Gonzalez faced the best closing pitcher in baseball, Mariano Rivera, with a chance to win the World Series.

By this point in Arizona's comeback, I was cheering for the home team. I wanted to see a base hit win the game. Gonzalez hit the ball up the middle, scoring Jay Bell from third for the winning run. The game wasn't technically over until Bell touched home plate, but I knew it was over as the ball left Gonzalez's bat. I had been cheering for the Diamondbacks as the pitch was delivered, but when the ball reached the outfield and the game was over, my thoughts turned elsewhere. I immediately felt bad for New York and all the fans there. I could tell that all the other pages had the same feeling because the cheers lasted only a second, and then we realized that Arizona's win meant that New York had lost.

It was a sad feeling for a moment, but New York had clearly proven itself to be bigger than baseball by this point. For every Derek Jeter and Bernie Williams, there were dozens of firefighters and police officers to admire. New Yorkers would have understood who their real heroes were even if the Yankees had pulled off another victory. Baseball players could not compare to those who were working tirelessly to clean up the hallowed Ground Zero, and no one could compare to those heroes who had made that site their final resting place.

America didn't need a sports victory for a New York dynasty. America needed a great baseball game in which athletes acted out that scenario that we all pretend to be in while playing in our backyards as kids. We needed a moment like a game-winning hit in Game 7 exactly because it was trivial. For one evening we could look on and make heroes out of athletes playing a game. We had to take a break from our vigilant concern over terrorism and relax for a while to share these great moments and celebrate them as a country. A fantastic Game 7 did not directly lead to the defeat of a terrorist, but it did allow us to take our minds elsewhere for a moment, only to come back more resolved.

Senator John McCain came to the floor of the U.S. Senate to congratulate the Arizona Diamondbacks on a great season. Senator Tom Harkin (D-IA) took a break from his speech regarding the farm bill to yield the floor momentarily to McCain. As McCain spoke, he made a reference to the gallery, and when I looked up I saw some of the players from the Arizona team. I recognized the pitchers Randy Johnson and Curt Schilling immediately. Many of the pages were excited by the celebrities visiting the gallery. McCain provided an interesting change of pace from the politics of the day by taking a couple of minutes to congratulate the new baseball champions.

When McCain yielded the floor back to Harkin, the Senator from Iowa gave a token congratulations wish to the team as well, but he seemed to want to get right back to business on his farm bill. Some of the pages saw the Diamondback players leave the gallery, and the chase began. A few pages had cameras with them, so they left the Senate floor and tracked down Randy Johnson and other players for pictures. I'm sure these pages meant no insult to Senator Harkin's speech, but it's not too often you get to meet world class baseball players in the Capitol!

Music shone through as another form of American popular culture that created inspiration for post-9/11 life. Ironically, it was an Irish band that recorded an album that swept across America. The band U2 won three Grammy Awards in 2001 and went on to win four more at the 2002 ceremony. All seven awards were given for U2's work on the album *All That You Can't Leave Behind.*

A few days after September 11th, some of the Senate pages down the hall from me played the U2 CD early in the morning as we got ready for a day of school and work. I remember liking U2's music before that day, but the optimistic message of the song "Beautiful Day" won me over as a dedicated fan of lead singer Bono and his band mates. The message of the song was winning over all the pages within earshot. Even after all we had been through in the past days, we couldn't help but smile as Bono sang, "It's a beautiful day. / Don't let it get away." The song had been out for a while by this point, but hearing it on that morning made all the difference.

I spoke with my roommate Jay Wright about U2 and soon found out that he was a huge fan. His endorsement led me to look into the band further, and then I purchased the CD for myself. When I listen to "Beautiful Day," I can't help but think back to the beautiful morning in September that turned so ugly. It had been a picture-perfect day with a blue sky and a pleasant temperature, but little else about that day could be considered beautiful. The days I have in mind when I listen to the words of that song are the days that followed the attacks when the country united and the Congress returned to work in the Capitol. I often think back to that morning when some Senate pages played the song and united our group with a sense of optimism. These ideas of unity and optimism created many beautiful days, and hopefully we won't "let it get away."

Another phrase in the song reads, "What you don't have, you don't need it now. / What you don't know, you can feel it somehow." For me, the first line carried a sense of necessary self-sufficiency. I could use whatever assets I had at my disposal and whatever character traits I had developed to make it through this difficult time, but if God hadn't blessed me with something by this point, I must not have needed it. I had a great group of new friends, a supportive family back in South Dakota, and an understanding of the importance of freedom and democracy. This was about all I had for standing up against terror, and it was all I needed.

While the first line carried a message of confidence, the second line conveyed a sense of the unknown and a feeling of doubt. This line reminds me of a message communicated by Defense Secretary Rumsfeld regarding intelligence and the War on Terror. He claimed that there are three sub-groups of information: known knowns, known unknowns, and unknown unknowns. After September 11th all of us knew there was enemy trying to kill Americans. That was a known known. However, many of the details, such as the location of Osama bin Laden, were known unknowns. We knew that bin Laden was responsible for the attacks and that he was out there somewhere, but we didn't know exactly where. The final category is the scariest in this new war. Unknown unknowns could not be predicted, but at the same time, what we didn't know we could "feel it somehow." We didn't know if and when there would be another attack, and we certainly had not predicted anthrax through the mail, yet we did have an under-standing, a feeling, that the post-9/11 world required us to expect the un-expected and respond as well as we could.

The other U2 song I frequently listen to is "Walk On." This song won a Grammy for record of the year in February 2002. While the music sends a great message of perseverance, "Walk On" and "Beautiful Day" were both written long before the attacks of September 2001. U2 could not have known the way their lyrics would take on a life of their own, inspiring my-self and others to strengthen in resolve at a time when we truly needed it. In "Walk On" Bono sang the chorus that inspired so many lovers of freedom:

> *Walk on, walk on*
> *What you got they can't steal it*
> *No, they can't even feel it*
> *Walk on, walk on*
> *Stay safe tonight*

The terrorists can't steal our freedom, but we can surrender it to them if we don't persevere. I also like this chorus because it seems to focus on taking one day at a time. It pleads with us only to "walk on." It doesn't

ask us to cover a certain distance or move at a quick pace; it only asks for
continued forward progress. While serving as a page, I loved the line "stay
safe tonight" because it was a symbol that I had made it through another
day, and I would get up and do it all over again the next day.

Another portion of the song acknowledged the hardships on all of us
in America as we entered this war:

> *And I know it aches, how your heart it breaks*
> *You can only take so much*
> *Walk on, walk on*

On bad days these lines would bring tears to my eyes, but the simple
idea of walking on was extraordinary. My heart would break for others as
they had rough days, and I had my own share of difficult days. Jen Cohen's
determination to get through her ordeal after the anthrax attack showed
how a commitment to the page program was a simple idea but not an easy
one to follow through on. We would all have moments where we had to
stop and ask ourselves how much we could really take, but invariably we
chose to walk on. It is exactly what the terrorists don't want us to do. They
hope we stop our progress, become complacent, or better yet, attempt ap-
peasement by giving in to their demands. All the pages continued to walk
to work each day despite the terrorists' threats, and after the anthrax attacks we would "walk on" past the Hart Building and continue to defy the
terrorists.

Soon after my time as a page was complete, I learned that Bono had
made a trip to Capitol Hill. One of the proctors sent out an e-mail telling
all the pages of my class that the new group of Senate pages had gotten
to meet him! I was so jealous! I had heard of Bono's occasional visits to
Capitol Hill, so I had hoped he might make a visit before I left in January.
Bono is a strong advocate for the continent of Africa on issues like debt
and AIDS. Another interesting fact I learned while in Washington was the
friendship between Senator Jesse Helms and Bono. This made for an odd
pairing between a conservative U.S. Senator in his eighties and a rock star
campaigning for relatively liberal causes.

A final area of popular culture to examine is television. All the pages loved to watch the news to see how the media covered the actions of the U.S. Senate, so Fox News and CNN were frequently watched. We could only take so much news, though, so we tried to unwind with other entertaining shows. The shows that we found entertaining probably weren't what the average teenager liked to watch. We had an interest in all things political, so even during a show like *The Simpsons*, a political joke would win us over quickly.

I remember watching *The Simpsons* with Jay quite a bit. We were both pretty big fans of the show and its humor. You might be thinking that this sounds like a normal show for a group of teenagers to be watching, but our favorite scene gives us away as Senate pages. A group of us nearly died from laughter at a scene featuring the Springfield Republicans, which included the fictional Montgomery Burns, as well as real-life politicians Bob Dole and Strom Thurmond. The reference to the ancient Senator Thurmond must have gone over the heads of many kids our age, but we could appreciate it from first-hand knowledge of the man.

The television program that had the most faithful following among many of the Senate pages was *The West Wing*. Although this political drama focused on a different branch of government than our area of expertise, many of us found it fascinating. The series was at its height of popularity after hitting the scene in 1999. The concept of the show was fantastic, and the writing was outstanding. Both the Republicans and the Democrats in our group loved the show. In my case, it didn't hurt that the Democratic President Josiah Bartlett, played by Martin Sheen, was a big Notre Dame fan!

It was interesting to watch the show follow real world events like terrorism. The season premiere was delayed a few weeks after the terrorist attacks. *The West Wing* aired a special episode in early October throughout which all the characters essentially gave independent monologues on terrorism. It was a great episode, giving viewers some insight into the feelings of each character and providing a stimulus for much more discussion on the subject in households across our country.

Still, some of the avid fans in the group were growing restless as the show's season premiere continued to be delayed. It was mid-October before we were able to jump into the third season of *The West Wing*. We understood that it was tasteful to delay the high-impact, fast-paced political drama for a few weeks to let the nation recover from the shell shock of 9/11. Still, it was frustrating to be held back from a television event that we had been anticipating since the previous season's finale. Once the third season hit full swing, we looked forward to Wednesday evenings all week. I always hoped that I wouldn't have to work late on those nights, so I could get home and watch the latest episode.

All these elements of popular culture shaped part of the world we lived in back in the fall of 2001. Sports, music, and television play some role in all of our lives, and sometimes we use them as escapes from the daily grind. I found it important to take a deep breath every once in a while, sit down in front of the TV, and think about absolutely nothing. With the stress of work and school running high, it was necessary to take a break from it all at some points.

I could feel that we had entered a new world after the terrorist attacks, though, because we saw a lot of our entertainment through a new prism. We appreciated all these beautiful elements of our culture that much more when our way of life came under attack. Sports heroes were still recognized for their achievements, yet they were only heroes in sports. We had learned what real heroes were all about in New York City—not at Yankee Stadium, but at the World Trade Center.

Teeny bopper tunes and defamatory rap lyrics took a back seat to an Irish band that filled the void in the time of America's need. The music of U2, which would have been considered good regardless of the terrorist attacks, could now be considered important in inspiring a nation to persevere for the cause of freedom.

Television provided news, comedy, and drama. *The West Wing* brought its audience into the White House for a taste of what an administration must go through when the country hits crisis mode. The show also provided an entertaining stimulus for people to discuss political issues without having to tune into C-SPAN and listen to real politicians.

All these examples of popular culture, which could have provided excuses for us to put our heads in the sand and escape the bitter realities of terrorism for a while longer, instead served to unite a nation with a sense of optimism. We opened up to one another and decided that a life of actively defending freedom was preferable to a life of shrinking away in fear. This phenomenon shows that freedom works. The rights of free speech and free press allowed our citizens to come to the correct conclusion that we had something worth defending. The terrorists may hate free expression because of the dissidence that comes along with it, but the West embraces these freedoms because the cream will rise to the top when it is most needed. The right ideas will prevail because they are right. The ideas based in terror will fail because those who have tasted freedom will never give it up for a life of fear.

Chapter 14
Meet the Birdwells

Soon after celebrating a quick and quiet Thanksgiving back home in South Dakota, I returned to Washington, D.C., to learn another lesson about what I could be thankful for that year. On December 4, 2001, a group of Senate Pages got the chance to visit U.S. Army Lieutenant Colonel Brian Birdwell. Brian was severely burned in the terrorist attack on the Pentagon. He reminded all of us of the terrible violence of September 11th. The sight of his injuries made me all the more thankful that the Capitol Building was spared because more deaths and severe injuries like his surely would have occurred. I was also thankful for the chance to meet a family that had been inspired by God to live their lives with optimism rather than retreat into self-pity.

The principal of the Senate Page School, Mrs. Weeden, had learned of Brian's story and begun correspondence with him and his wife, Mel. Mrs. Weeden informed the Birdwells that the Senate pages would love to come to visit Brian at the hospital or do anything else to help lift his spirit during the difficult recovery process. Our page class had effectively "adopted" Brian as our own. Many of the pages wrote him notes or letters of encouragement, and others brought back fun trinkets from their home states as gifts to the soldier and his family.

Another symbolic action we took to support the Birdwells occurred in the Senate Page Student Council. I had the honor of being elected vice president of my class and drafting a resolution honoring the courage of

Lieutenant Colonel Birdwell. Jay had been elected president of our student council, so he called on me to read the resolution for all the other pages to hear at a council meeting one morning immediately following classes. I remember reading it with a lot of pride, and then experiencing an even prouder moment as Jay called for the vote and the resolution passed unanimously. We all understood that we were only the Senate Page Student Council, not the U.S. Senate, but the symbolic effort was the least we could do.

In early December Mrs. Weeden announced a chance to go visit Brian at the hospital where he was recovering from his burns. A few pages had already been to the hospital to deliver Halloween pumpkins to the burn victims. Now I would get my turn to visit. Mrs. Weeden took about ten of us up to the hospital, and none of us really knew what to expect. I had never visited a burn victim before, let alone a severe burn victim from the terrorist attacks of September 11th. I had a sense of uneasiness, wondering how bad he would look. I also had a sense of awe as I thought, "What am I supposed to say to a guy who survived getting hit by an airliner on September 11th?"

Much of my anxiety was set aside immediately because Brian had a great sense of humor. He and his wife welcomed us into his hospital room. A Texas Longhorns flag hung in the room, and Brian talked about being from Texas. He was in a jovial mood and seemed excited to have a group of guests. It was an amazing first impression of a man who had been through so much pain, and in fact was still experiencing pain, yet could display such good spirits.

By this point Brian had moved far enough along in his recovery process that he would be leaving the hospital soon. The second- and third-degree burns that had covered approximately 60 percent of his body had been healing slowly but surely. His forehead was covered with the obvious marks of still healing skin grafts. His hands were covered with gloves to protect them. Bits of his ears were missing. He didn't look too bad, but we also understood that he had come a long way in the nearly three months since the attacks. Every day nurses would go through the painful process of removing his bandages and applying fresh ones to prevent infection. The most painful moments would occur when Brian had to take baths to clean off the dead skin. In the weeks following September 11th, with his life still in jeopardy, Brian had also gone through many surgeries as doctors tried to repair his burns and graft skin onto burnt portions of his body. Now, he looked thin and brittle, but his survival was no longer in doubt. Although it would take months to get out of the woods completely, the moment of American Flight 77's impact on the Pentagon would be the very closest Brian came to death.

In what he can explain only through divine intervention, Brian had left his office for the mundane task of using the restroom just moments before the plane hit his section of the Pentagon. This saved his life. He was in the process of returning to his office when the hallway in front of him exploded. He was knocked down by the fireball that ensued. He remembers the awful smell of jet fuel and the difficulty of escaping the fire. Brian came within minutes of dying from a combination of burns and smoke inhalation.

Brian explained the amazing role his faith played in his life. He was a religious man before, during, and after the attacks of September 11th. He told us all that it was a miracle that he had survived the explosion in the Pentagon, and he gives credit for that miracle to God. The pain of the initial burns, the pain of the baths, and the pain of the physical therapy all provided moments when he wondered why he hadn't just died and gotten it over with. These thoughts came only briefly, though, because he was patient and faithful enough to wait for God to show his reasons for keeping him alive.

Two great reasons God would have for keeping Brian alive were his roles as a great husband and father. Not coincidentally, Brian's wife and son were also two reasons that he survived. Mel was a pillar of strength that Brian needed for support as they grew together in love and faith during a time that could have crushed most people. His son, Matt, had a quiet strength about him. He was shy and reserved, but one could see that he loved his parents dearly and was doing his best to look out for them. Matt was only 12 at the time of the attacks, but he grew up quickly and faced the tragedy of his father's injuries with courage and remarkable understanding.

Matt went with the Senate pages on a field trip to Philadelphia. We took many field trips that we sarcastically designated as "mandatory fun" because on many weekends some of us would rather have slept all day than taken a road trip anywhere. The Philadelphia trip was different, though. We would see the Army/Navy football game, which was a time-honored rivalry. The cadets would prevail over the midshipmen on this occasion by a score of 26-17. Matt was pleased with the game, as he was obviously cheering for his father's branch of the military. My roommate Adam Anthony was one of the pages who stayed with Matt and really got to know him, and I could tell that Matt appreciated this effort.

Matt appreciated all of our support, but I could also tell that he was a bit shy. He would talk with Adam quite a bit, but I don't remember getting too much out of him. When I did speak with Matt, he seemed to be a fun-loving kid. He really enjoyed the bus ride, the game, and the opportunity to hang out with some older kids. I'm sure he knew that his dad was in the middle of a heroic recovery, but he was too modest to speak of how strong his family had been through it all. He simply accepted our compliments and our support and enjoyed a beautiful December day at Veterans Stadium.

I remember it being relatively warm for the first day of December. I also remember losing a bet with Jen Cohen on the outcome of the game! I will never forget the cadets and midshipmen marching on the field before the start of the game. These would be the new officers leading the way in a new kind of war. These men and women were part of our generation, the generation that would fight and win the War on Terror. As these cadets and midshipmen battled back and forth on the field and in entertaining skits played on the stadium's video board, one could get a sense of the intense spirit of the rivalry. Although these young men and women had been ingrained with the slogans of "Beat Army" and "Beat Navy" as if that sports victory were the sole goal of their institution, they also realized that the world had changed three months previous to this gridiron match-up. One couldn't help but cheer for both sides with the feeling that we were all on the same team. The commander in chief was present at the game, and he displayed that spirit by switching sides of the field ceremoniously at half-time, showing equal support for each branch of the service.

This was an amazing image of President Bush as he made the trip across the football field at the height of his popularity as commander in chief. This was a great moment for the President, but my favorite image of the President was illustrated by the words of Mel Birdwell in her and Brian's book *Refined by Fire*. It is a story that I will never forget because I know it is an experience that Bush will never forget.

George W. and Laura Bush made a trip to the burn unit in Washington, D.C., a couple days after September 11th to visit the victims of the attack on the Pentagon. Laura entered Brian's room first and spoke with Mel for a bit before the President arrived. When the President came into the room, he acknowledged Brian with a salute. Mel noticed the tired look and blood-shot eyes of a man with the weight of the world on his shoulders. Mel was understandably star-struck at the time and amazed that the commander in chief would salute a lower-ranking officer, but it got better. As Bush began to lower his salute, Brian began a feeble attempt to return the salute. This brought tears to Bush's eyes, and he held the salute until Brian finished his own three-quarter effort that revealed the red muscle of his skinless arm. The wounds were incredible, and it was amazing that Brian could raise his arm that far before the pain was too much. Bush then dropped his salute, completing the honor reserved for superiors rather than subordinates. If you watch the President get off his helicopter or plane, you will notice two members of the military holding their salute for the President well after he finishes the gesture. In a reversal of protocol, Bush had held his salute for this lieutenant colonel as a huge symbol of respect.

Bush then told Brian that he was a great hero. He also gave Brian and Mel a message of his resolve to take this fight to those who had per-petrated these horrible acts. He assured them that the attacks would not go unanswered. This moment and moments like it with the other families

had to have been the most difficult times for Bush. He carried the weight
of a nation in offering his condolences to the wounded and their families.
Yet this was Bush at his best. Bush didn't have to visit those victims. If
he chose to visit, he could have brought the press along for a great pho-
to op, or he could have just gone through the motions and gotten out of
there. He chose not only to visit the wounded, but to care for them as well.
The President and his wife showed an empathy and compassion that truly
reflected the feelings of the American public as a whole. The American
people had genuine feelings of sadness, anger, compassion, and love with
respect to the entire situation after September 11th. President Bush did his
job well by showing each of these emotions. It allowed all of us to relate to
the President, and the President to relate to us.

This story of Bush's salute to Brian in his hospital room remains the
greatest image I have of Bush despite (or possibly because of) the lack of
pictures of the event. In much the same way the President did, I stood in
front of Brian as he lay in a hospital bed. I had the same tears come to my
eyes as I recognized a hero before me. The only difference was that Brian
had recovered a lot in the weeks since the President's visit, so I saw a much
more healed hero.

The only image I can compare this to would be Bush's defining moment
on top of the rubble of Ground Zero when he proclaimed to the crowd, "I
can hear you. The rest of the world hears you, and the people who knocked
these buildings down will hear from all of us soon." This is my favorite
of Bush's public quotes, but this private meeting with the Birdwells had
much the same message. The salute symbolized Bush's understanding of
the great sacrifice Brian had made. Bush could "hear" Brian. His assurance to Brian that these attacks would not go unanswered meant that the
terrorists would soon understand the mighty resolve of the Birdwells and
the rest of the American people.

All of these emotions flashed in front of me during the visit with Brian
and Mel. I had learned of this gripping story of Bush's visit, so I understood what an honor it was that I had the chance to visit this hero as well.
The other amazing part of my visit was the appreciation we pages received

from Brian and Mel. I couldn't have imagined getting treated any better by such a great family unless I had been the President himself! This was a humble family that survived together with the power of prayer. Brian had taken the pressure off our visit with his sense of humor, and Mel did most of the rest of the talking with the strength of a saint. She explained to us all the things Brian had to go through, from surgeries to physical therapy, and we could tell that she felt the pain almost as much as Brian did.

Both repeatedly made references to the "miracle" that allowed Brian to still be alive. The amazing circumstances that had to go just right for Brian to survive from the moment of impact through the countless surgeries led the Birdwells to recognize a divine hand in the process. Much like my own feelings for how the Capitol Building was spared destruction, Brian sees his survival as a sign of God's grace on what was otherwise a day full of evil. Their faith was as strong as any I had ever witnessed. It would have been so easy to blame God for all the horrendous pain. It would have been easy to ask God why it had to be Brian's side of the Pentagon that was hit.

The Birdwells did the exact opposite. They praised God for keeping Brian alive. They valued life above all else and fought through any pain to maintain it. They also thanked God that the plane had hit the side of the Pentagon that it did because that side had been under renovation and was sparsely populated at the time. The Birdwells understood that Brian would have been safe if the plane had hit somewhere else, but many more people would have died. This is a family that sees and understands the big picture.

The Birdwells reminded me of Lisa Beamer. Lisa knew that her husband and the other passengers of Flight 93 saved lives in Washington, D.C., by sacrificing themselves. Lisa and Mel each experienced such different circumstances that a person could not judge which situation would be more difficult. Lisa had the comfort that her husband had been a hero and died on impact with no pain; however, Todd was dead, and that finality is crushing. Mel had to deal with the horrific injuries of her husband, but there was a hope for his survival.

I see it as no coincidence that these two women relied on the same thing as the solution to the two unique sets of circumstances that changed their lives. Lisa looked to God to find peace and to know that she would see Todd again one day in heaven. Mel looked to God for the strength to continue fighting for her husband's recovery from life-threatening burns. Both women understood that they had no direct control over the situations into which their husbands were placed on September 11th. They could only move forward with positive thoughts and guidance from a higher power.

Meeting the Birdwells was an incredible experience for me. It does wonders for the soul to meet a family that came to the brink of losing so much but fought back with all the courage they could muster. Brian was the first and only victim of the terrorist attacks I encountered while serving as a Senate page. His body had been weakened by the terrorists, but after speaking with him, I had little doubt that his spirit had been strengthened by the experience. Although his recovery process has been largely successful, he will always carry noticeable physical scars from his initial wounds. These scars will forever remind him of the pain he went through in the days, weeks, and months after the terrorist attacks. Brian, the person, reminds us all of the strength of the human spirit to overcome any physical wounds.

The Birdwells have used their strength not only to get through their own ordeal, but also to reach out to others. As Brian retired from the Army, he and his wife formed an organization to help other burn victims find their own courage to make it through the recovery process. Face the Fire Ministries helps burn victims and wounded servicemen find physical and spiritual healing. I encourage you to learn more about this amazing family, their story, and their charity by reading *Refined by Fire*. The Birdwells are great Americans who take little credit for themselves, but direct it all to their savior Jesus Christ instead. While they are thankful for all the help of the medical staff in Washington and the support of others like the Senate pages, they know that the ultimate thanks goes to the Great Physician who has the power to heal all wounds.

As we pages left the hospital that day, each of us had been inspired to try a little harder and complain a little less. We had had a demanding life during our time as pages, but our meeting with Brian and Mel put some things into perspective. Another thought came to many of our minds but was not discussed out loud. Circumstances could have been different that day in September. What if Flight 77 had had the Capitol as its target instead of the Pentagon? What if Flight 93 had reached its target rather than crashing in a field in Pennsylvania? The answers to these questions involved imagining ourselves or our friends in a hospital bed, terribly injured, like our new hero Lieutenant Colonel Brian Birdwell.

That was part of the reason Brian was a hero to us. With the knowledge that the Capitol was a target just like the Pentagon was, I could imagine the possibility of being in the same position as Brian. I couldn't imagine, however, the strength it would take to make it through that situation alive and recover despite all the pain. It would be easy to give up. It would be easy to lose faith. The Birdwells didn't give up or lose faith, though, so they were a shining example to all of us.

The other reason Brian was a hero to us and the rest of America was his status as a member of the military. These people put themselves on the line every day for the purpose of securing our lives and our freedoms. By the time we visited Brian at the hospital, he and the other Pentagon victims were no longer the only military casualties in the war on terror. Taking the war to Afghanistan had its cost, and soldiers were being killed and wounded.

This thought takes me back to the image of President Bush standing over the severely burned lieutenant colonel. The mind of the commander in chief was weighted with knowledge that this was only the beginning. What many may have predicted as an uneventful or domestic-oriented presidency was now an administration in which the leader of the free world was at war. Brian would not be the last injured soldier that the President would meet. Mel would not be the last grieving wife that the President would console. Bush would handle the roles of consoler in chief and commander in chief well as the nation simultaneously grieved and looked for a way to make sure these dreadful attacks would never be repeated on American soil.

The final inspiration that the pages took from our visit with the Birdwells was the call to service. I remember having a conversation with one page on the drive from the hospital about the possibility of entering the military through the Reserve Officer Training Corps (ROTC) program in college. It would be a great way to pay for school and serve the country. The main reason this page had thought seriously about the military was the idea of being part of a team.

"Being a page has really made me feel like a part of something bigger. I feel that I can do more good as one part of a larger team. That's the same feeling I get from the idea of military service," he said. It was a feeling that all the pages were beginning to have. Events like the 9/11 attacks and the anthrax attacks made us all realize we were in a battle for our very lives, and we were in it together. We only had a little over a month left in our service to the U.S. Senate, and for most of us it was a question of how, not if, we would serve our country again.

I thank God for the chance to have met the Birdwell family. Matt taught me the amazing power of quiet strength. Mel taught me the importance of an unyielding commitment to loved ones. Brian taught me a great lesson in perseverance and determination. It is painful just to think about what Brian went through physically and mentally, but it is more painful to think about a world where families like this one, with their optimism and faith, don't exist. The Birdwells teach us all the importance of service to God, country, and family.

Heroes like Lieutenant Colonel Brian Birdwell don't come along every day, but their stories should be remembered every day. Our lives depend on it.

CHAPTER 15
CHRISTMAS 2001

December 20, 2001, would be the last day the U.S. Senate would be in session during my service as a page. I would head home for the holidays and return on January 2, 2002. We pages would still go to work in the Capitol, but we would be able to concentrate on school work because there would be little else for us to do. Ironically, one of my fears early on in the program had been that Congress would recess for the year in October, and I would be bored the rest of my time in Washington. To the contrary, this Congress worked well into December and would pick up again in late January.

It took a while to grasp the realization that I would never again see the U.S. Senate in action from the vantage point of a page. Watching the action on C-SPAN2 or even watching from the gallery would not be the same. After a few days at home with my family and friends, I started to realize that my life would never be the same, either.

Our English teacher, Mrs. Owens, told us in class one day that we "could never go home." Of course, she did not mean that we would be trapped in Webster Hall studying American literature forever. She pointed out the experience that many classes of Senate pages have gone through. The Senate page experience had made each of us grow up quickly and learn things in a new environment. For our class especially, these were experiences and lessons that our friends and family back home could never truly understand.

This was another reason that my group of Senate pages has had a special bond that has lasted well beyond our time together in the program. We found it hard to relate our stories to friends back home who may have been uninterested in politics. We found it hard to convey our feelings from 9/11 or the anthrax attacks to people who were hundreds of miles away from the events. A part of me has accepted what Mrs. Owens told us. I have come to terms with the fact that most people will never truly understand what it was like to be doing what I was doing at the time I was doing it. It is not the case that these people don't care or don't try to understand. It is just a case where full knowledge can only come from experience. The obvious analogy would be soldiers during a war. The other Senate pages are my own "band of brothers" (and sisters), and we made it through difficult times as juniors in high school. We could not expect people to understand everything we went through, and we could not expect everything at home to be just like we left it.

Going home for Christmas gave me a quick taste of what it would be like to come home for good a few weeks later in January. Mrs. Owens was right in the sense that South Dakota didn't push the pause button for me. Life went on. I celebrated Christmas with my dad. We drove to Aberdeen, the hometown of Senator Daschle, to visit my uncle John for the holiday. We did all the fun stuff with presents and the Christmas tree. We went to church as a family in Aberdeen and thanked God for the time we could spend together. I spent the remaining days of my Christmas break with my mom and step-dad. I rested up as best I could for the final three weeks of the semester and studied for final exams.

The kids at my high school moved along in their curriculum, doing different things than I was doing at my school in Washington. Everyone had changed a little bit from the way I remembered them. Of course, I felt like I had changed a lot and grown up a lot in the past months, so it was all relative. I could even sense a difference in my own family. My parents looked at me a bit differently. They really began to treat me more as an equal than as a kid. I was being recognized as a young adult who had managed to be fairly self-sufficient for a significant period of time.

So it seemed like Mrs. Owens was right, as usual. We couldn't go home. Well, we couldn't go to a home where everyone and everything would be as we left it. We had changed, and others had changed. The frustrating part would be that neither side could truly understand what it was like to be in the shoes of the other without experiencing it first-hand. I don't think that that means the story should go untold, though. The message is too important. The symbolism is all too clear. The Senate pages represented the generation being tasked with a great mission. Friends and family back home asked all of us about our experiences because they understood the importance of this great mission. They had not experienced what we had experienced, but anyone who witnessed the attacks of September 11th understood the stakes involved. People began to ask the question: "Can this generation stack up to the Greatest Generation and complete this task?"

I could already feel the interest in my story and the Senate page story during my short Christmas break. Most of the questions came from family and friends, but months later I would begin speaking with more and more people who recognized the symbolism of this group of young people standing strong during a perilous time in our nation's history. The sense of unity that I could feel back home in South Dakota inspired me that much more to get back to Washington and finish the job that we had started on September 4, 2001.

As much as I looked forward to Christmas break and seeing my family, I missed all my Senate page friends after being home for a few days. It was a small taste of how hard it would be to leave the program for good on January 18, 2002. I tried to make the most of my time at home by relaxing and studying, but I actually spent most of my energy getting over a cough. I had survived September evacuations and October anthrax, but some little cousins in Aberdeen had finally penetrated my immune system! The cough cleared up in time for me to board the plane back to Washington feeling pretty well.

All of the pages reunited at Webster Hall for the final push. We had little work to do besides studying for final exams, so we tried to have as much fun as we could. One day at work we were allowed to create our own mock Senate in the empty U.S. Senate chamber. I had the privilege of standing at Senator Daschle's desk and addressing all of my fellow pages. Most of the other pages stood behind their own Senators' desks, spoke of how much they had enjoyed their time in Washington, and said some goodbyes to the rest of the pages.

Jason Frerichs stood behind South Dakota Senator Tim Johnson's desk and told the group something very important. He told us to go home and "share our story." Jason encouraged us to discuss our experience with our friends and neighbors and let them know of all the important work going on in Washington. We all understood what he meant, but it was easier said than done. In fact, it has taken a whole book just to tell my portion of "our story"! That has been the theme of my relationship with all the other pages, though. We were a team that made it through the Senate page experience together, and although there are 30 slightly different perspectives, it is still *our* story.

The final chapter of our collective story would be the closing ceremony on January 18, 2002. From that moment we would all go our separate ways, but we would forever have a bond that would keep us in touch with a sense of purpose. We shared an experience, and we shared an understanding. We experienced first-hand the beginnings of the conflict that our nation finds itself in today. We understood that we would be 30 among many in our generation who would take the lead in securing freedom for many more generations to come. We understood that the closing ceremony was the end of our careers as Senate pages, but it was only the beginning of our service to our country.

CHAPTER 16
SENATE PAGE
CLOSING CEREMONY

I didn't sleep much on my last night in Webster Hall. I was nervous about leaving the page program. I was nervous about all the events of the following day. As class vice president, I would have two speaking roles in the closing ceremony. First, I would recognize the Birdwell family, who would be in attendance. Second, I would introduce the two pages who had been selected to give keynote speeches.

Jay Wright would serve as master of ceremonies because of his status as class president. He had been working on his part for the past few days. He would lead the rest of the class into the Mansfield Room of the Capitol for the ceremony and introduce all of the speakers except for the two that I would introduce. Senators Conrad and Lott would be attending the ceremony and sharing some remarks with us, so Jay would be introducing them to the audience.

The audience was made up mainly of family members of the various pages. Christina came to watch the ceremony. We were all sad that she couldn't sit with us up front, but we were glad she had come to support us on that special day. Some staff members came to see the ceremony as well. The cloakroom staff people that we had worked with every day had gotten to know many of us pretty well, so it was nice to see that they had taken the time to see us on our final day as pages.

I woke up early that morning, showered, and got dressed quickly. I hadn't gotten much sleep, but I would be running on the adrenaline of the day's excitement anyway. Jay and I headed downstairs to discuss some last minute items with Mrs. Weeden. She looked over the text of what we were going to say and gave approval and encouragement. She told us that we had nothing to be nervous about because she knew we would do a great job.

I grabbed a quick breakfast and walked to the Capitol Building with Katie Ruedebusch. She would be leading the audience in the Pledge of Allegiance at the beginning of the ceremony. She had been elected secretary of the Senate Page Student Council, making South Dakota very well represented among class officers. It would be a fun experience for her because we had started each day's session with the Pledge, but it had always been led by the Senator serving as presiding officer. Now, Katie would get the chance to play this role and honor our flag before the two Senators and various staff honored our service as pages.

I reached the Mansfield Room, where Scott Moore and Jason Frerichs were practicing their speeches one last time before the guests would start filing into the room. I had a couple of last-minute questions for Mrs. Weeden. I asked her where the Birdwells would be seated, so I could become familiar with where I would be addressing some of my statements in the ceremony. As I began to leave the room, I heard a line of Scott's speech that forced an alteration of my own comments.

I had actually been trying to avoid listening to Scott and Jason because I wanted to hear their speeches for the first time during the ceremony. Scott made a comment, though, that directly contradicted something I had planned on saying when addressing our honored guests, the Birdwells. He argued that the terrorist attacks of September 11th did not define our page experience. I had planned on saying just the opposite as an introduction to the amazing story of Lieutenant Colonel Birdwell at the Pentagon.

I instantly thought, "Oh! I have to change the wording of my speech so we don't look stupid by contradicting one another." After listening to a bit more of Scott's speech and thinking about it myself some more, I realized that I would change the wording because Scott was right. I ended up emphasizing the importance of that day, but also stressing that we had not allowed those events to define us. Scott would go on to beautifully explain how we had worked hard and played hard to define ourselves, rather than letting any outside event define us. Also, if you met Scott and knew how smart he was, you would defer to his line of thinking as well!

After adjusting some semantics of my written remarks, I walked out into the hallway. The wait began. All of the pages stood in a single file line down the hall from the Mansfield Room well before the ceremony was set to start. We were all told to be there early, and if we weren't disciplined young adults by now, we never would be. So we waited, with Jay at the front of the line, followed by me, then the two keynote speakers, Scott and Jason. Everyone had knots in their stomachs because the end of this ceremony would mean the nearly instantaneous end of our careers as pages. A reception would follow in the LBJ Room of the Capitol, but pages and their families could leave the reception at any time and head home.

We had all taken time the night before to say most of our goodbyes. The proctors had provided each of us with a piece of poster board. We would sign each other's poster boards with messages on a different level than the usual high school yearbook "have a good summer" line. Every page and proctor took the time to write a unique message for each page, and I still cherish that poster board as a snapshot in time that reflects how much we all meant to each other. After that, since we were done with school and work, we horsed around for the rest of the evening in Webster Hall, making the most of our last night there. It would have been difficult enough to say goodbye just to Jen and my roommates, but I tried to speak with each of the pages individually and pledge to keep in touch as best we could. Obviously, one evening wasn't enough time to say goodbye to such great friends, friends who had really become a family.

The single file line broke down every so often into clumps of pages saying some more goodbyes or joking around to keep the mood upbeat. Some of the girls were crying. These were much different tears than these same girls had cried on September 11th. In that case they cried that they wanted to go home. Now their sadness came because we had made a new home together in Washington, and they didn't want to leave. I got a bit choked up myself when I left my position in line to talk to Jen Cohen once more before the ceremony started. After spending as much time together as we had over the past weeks, we didn't have to say much. She could tell that I was a bit nervous and gave me some encouragement. I could tell that she was getting over the side effects from her medicine and feeling better because of her beautiful smile in full form.

The page experience had tested Jen immensely, and she handled it all extremely well. She was ready to go home, though. She deserved the break from the madness of Washington. While I could sense some sadness in her eyes that we would be going our separate ways, she seemed excited about having her mother in attendance and about going home to be with the rest of her family.

I returned to my spot in the line behind Jay as one of our teachers told us we were almost ready to begin. Jay led the way into the room that we had all known as the place where the Republicans held their weekly lunches. Now it would serve as the location of our celebration for completing our service as Senate pages. About 15 chairs flanked each side of the podium and faced the audience. After all the pages had come to their positions at their assigned seats, Jay stepped forward to begin the ceremony.

Our ceremony followed the protocol that our 100 bosses would have greatly appreciated. We began by honoring God and country. Katie led us in the pledge of allegiance, and Senate Sergeant at Arms Al Lenhardt offered a prayer. These two activities were more than just going through the motions for us. We were sincere in our patriotism and in our service to the government. We were also sincere in our thankfulness to God for making it through all the difficult days that this service had required.

Jay moved forward again to the microphone to jump straight into his master of ceremonies role by introducing Senator Conrad. Conrad was a great speaker. He came to the floor every so often, mainly to speak on budgetary issues. That can be a bit of a dry subject, so this venue gave him the opportunity to be more personal. He joked around and praised us for sticking to our jobs through all the hard times. He even gave a plug to his page, Jen, for her perseverance.

Jay thanked Senator Conrad for his words and then proudly introduced the leader of the Republicans, Senator Lott. Jay had some fun with this one by introducing the Mississippi Senator as his "neighbor to the west." Sure, Jay was from Alabama, but Senator Lott greeted Jay like they were truly next-door neighbors. Lott was impressive when he addressed us pages and our families. He conveyed a strong message that he was optimistic about our nation's future. He said he hoped that our Senate page class was a true indication of our generation.

After the Senators had spoken, the four teachers of the Senate Page School came forward to present academic awards. Each teacher taught two variations of a core subject. For example, Mrs. Owens, the English teacher, taught American literature and composition. Therefore, a total of eight awards were given, with an award going to the top student in each class. Seven of the eight awards went to one room in Webster Hall. Kevin Burleson, Ryan Majerus, and Scott had two great things going for them academically: they were all naturally intelligent, and they had a quiet room where they focused on studying. Unfortunately, this meant that I had to explain to my mom that my roommates and I weren't quite as studious! Katie took home the only remaining award that the other guys didn't get.

My time in the event's program was soon upon me. I walked to the podium with a bit of nerves but relaxed more and more as I told the story of the Birdwell family. It meant a lot to us that they had made the effort to come to the closing ceremony. From their perspective, though, I'm sure they thought of it as normal reciprocity. They genuinely appreciated the support they had received from Mrs. Weeden and the Senate pages as Brian recovered from his burns. It was only natural for this great family to take the time to visit us that day in the Capitol.

I read the resolution that I had written and that the Senate Page Student Council had passed weeks earlier. I remember glancing at Senator Conrad as I announced that I would be reading the resolution. A part of me thought that a U.S. Senator might be amused at the thought of a resolution created by our group. I almost expected a condescending grin or a dismissive attitude toward my simple legislative effort. I knew better than that, though, because I had met with Senator Conrad, and I knew he was very supportive of all of our activities as Senate pages. That last bit of self-doubt was washed away when Senator Conrad nodded approvingly as I read the resolution.

"Whereas, the courage and determination of this nation to come together and heal is reflected in Lieutenant Colonel Birdwell's courage and determination to recuperate from his wounds," read an important clause of the resolution.

When I had finished reading the resolution, the entire room exploded with a loud ovation. While I had expected some applause, I had not expected the amazing enthusiasm of the audience. My previous self-doubt had not turned into a feeling of self-importance, however. I knew that the whole of the applause was for Brian and his family. I stepped back from the podium and clapped for a few seconds, as the sustained ovation prevented me from doing anything else.

As the audience quieted down, I made eye contact with Brian and acknowledged him one more time before moving on in the program by saying, "Thank you, sir." His response was simple enough in words, but his tone and body language conveyed a strong message that I will never forget. He looked me square in the eye, shook his head slightly, and forcefully said, "No, thank you."

He emphasized the word "you" but not to direct the comment to me and me alone. He meant for my message of thanks to be turned around and sent right back to me and all the Senate pages. Brian's words were a message on behalf of his family to my family, the Senate page family. The verbal and non-verbal signals added up to a message that hit me hard at the moment and brought tears to my eyes. His words were so genuine, as if to say, "You'll never know what this means to me and my family." He's right. I'll never understand all the pain that they went through. I'll never be able to quantify how much we helped the Birdwells by "adopting" Brian, talking with Mel, and bringing Matt on a road trip with us. I have little doubt, though, that it is a very small amount when compared with the amount of courage and unyielding faith that the Birdwells mustered on their own account.

All these emotions zipped through me as Brian floored me with his graciousness, but I gathered myself by taking a deep breath and moved to the next item that I was responsible for in the program. I would introduce our keynote speakers. Jason would be speaking first, and I had fun introducing my fellow South Dakotan. His speech was full of colorful stories and inspiring anecdotes that related to our time as pages and our future as America's next leaders.

Jason had grown up on a farm in South Dakota and believed that a sense of optimism was necessary in farming and in politics. He began with a funny story about the power that optimism has over one's attitude. "I know a story about a Little League baseball player and optimism," Jason started. "During one of his first ball games, this little ballplayer was in the outfield when his dad came to watch the game. His dad was close enough to his boy to ask him, 'What's the score?' The boy hollered out, 'Twenty-two to nothing!' His dad said, 'I suppose you're kind of disappointed with a score like twenty-two to nothing?'"

One might expect a whiny response of a kid ready to quit baseball for good, but the character in Jason's story replies, "Oh, no. We haven't been up to bat yet. Just wait until we get up to bat!" This got a good laugh from the crowd in the Mansfield Room, and Jason continued his speech with a few more stories and some praise for all the hard work the pages had put in during the past semester. He finished with a story with a great message about the future, especially when combined with his sense of optimism throughout the speech.

Jason recounted a tale of wise old man and a little boy. The little boy would try to fool the old man with riddles but could never succeed. One day the little boy thought he had found the way to fool the wise old man. He caught a bird and held it in his hands. The little boy would ask the old man if the bird was dead or alive. If the old man said that the bird was alive, the boy would kill the bird with his hands, then open them to reveal a dead bird. If the old man said that the bird was dead, the boy would open his hands, and the bird would fly away. The boy found the man and posed his riddle with bird in his hands. He asked the old man, "Is the bird dead or alive?" The wise old man pondered this question for a moment and said, "It's in your hands; it's as you'll have it."

Jason related the bird to our future and gave us a sense of purpose in molding that future as he concluded, "Our future and the future of our great country is in our hands; it is as we will have it." I stood and shook Jason's hand on my way back to the podium as the audience rewarded his effort with a round of applause.

My last speaking role in the ceremony would be to introduce Scott for his keynote address. I was excited to hear his speech in entirety after having fortunately caught a certain portion of it earlier in the morning. After hearing a few sentences of his speech, I had high expectations for the rest of it. Having known Scott for a while, I knew it was impossible to overestimate his abilities, and he delivered above and beyond expectations yet again with this effort.

Like Jason, Scott got a laugh early on in his speech. Scott summed up some of the staples of the Senate page experience by saying, "Long days spent on the rostrum or searching for obscure and occasionally non-existent basement offices have made the Capitol something of a second home for us. Shared laughter in the Senate lobby, shared meal vouchers, and the magic of looking out onto the Mall during late-night amendment runs has captured something in all of us."

The punch line came as Scott made a witty observation about our soon-to-be status as ex-government employees. "These things and many others will now be forever a part of us, as will the right to stand on the Mall and casually inform tourists gawking at the Capitol, 'Yeah, I used to work there,'" he said with mock arrogance. After this laugh and reminder that we would have bragging rights for the rest of our lives, Scott transitioned to his message about how the 9/11 attacks had affected our lives.

"Suddenly this work was not merely stapling and copying and errand-running, but the work of a nation. We became something altogether different from the pages of September 10th," Scott claimed. "It was the pride that, even in our small role, we were doing something other than being afraid, something that made this country strong in spite of our wounded hearts."

I found this to be an amazing selection of words, and Scott's delivery was great on two levels. An outsider could tell that everything he said was from his heart and that he was speaking on behalf of all of his fellow pages as he said it. The next section of his speech was the part that I had heard earlier in the morning.

"One of the more amazing things about this page class is that, as tremendous as September 11th was for us, it has not defined our experience. We may all be changed because of it, but in the best tradition of pages, we have not let it interfere with good times," Scott said and then proceeded to list a bunch of inside jokes and other fun times the pages had experienced together. Now the laughter was coming up front from all the pages, as we knew what Scott was talking about. Then Scott made the strongest statement of his speech, "We have become the pages that not only survived September 11th, but thrived in spite of it."

Scott concluded his speech by addressing his fellow Senate pages directly. "We have become something special during our five months in the Capitol. We have become pages, something that very few have ever done. We leave with many wonderful memories and many wonderful friends. But we will never forget what it feels like to sit on the rostrum and look out to see history made every day. We will all leave a piece of our hearts on the Senate floor."

This last sentence touched all of us because it was true. A piece of us would always be with the Senate. Luckily for us, a piece of the Senate would come home with us. The carpet on the Senate floor was being redone in the final weeks of our term, so the staff had arranged to get a framed square of the old carpet for each page. All of the pages were called alphabetically to come forward and receive not only a certificate for completing the program, but also a piece of the Senate floor.

Jay and I received two final awards. Mrs. Weeden awarded Jay with the Senate Page Student Council Award for his management of the council as president and his great work with the organization of the closing ceremony. She then gave me the Leadership Award for my efforts as vice president. Jay and I sat back down and glanced at each other. It was a look that conveyed a lot of messages. We had shared a room and a growing friendship since September 2, 2001. We had worked on opposite sides of the aisle in the Senate, but worked together on almost everything else. Student Council was one forum among many in which we got along and accomplished some things worth recognizing at the closing ceremony. As we nodded congratulations to each other on our awards, I could tell that we were each more proud of the other than we were of ourselves. That was a great feeling.

As the ceremony ended, everyone was invited to another room in the Capitol for refreshments and the painful process of saying goodbye. All the pages and their families made their way to the LBJ Room, where the Democrats have their weekly caucus lunches. I gave my family a tour of the Senate floor and lobby along the way. They were pretty impressed with the place, and I couldn't help recalling Scott's great quote, "Yeah, I used to work there!"

All of the pages gathered in the LBJ Room to take a picture with Brian Birdwell. He looked a little better than when I had visited him in the hospital. He still wore gloves to protect his hands, and he wore a headband to protect the skin healing on his forehead. After we took the picture, I brought my family over to meet him. As I approached, he stuck out his gloved right hand and greeted me with excitement. He took pleasure in meeting my family, and I was so happy to get the chance to exchange a few last words with him before leaving Washington.

I began the process of saying goodbye to all the pages, teachers, and staff members while also introducing them to my parents. It was hard to find the words then, and it is hard to find the words now, to express what each of these individuals meant to me for that wonderful period of time. All we could do was pledge to stay in touch, and for the most part we have.

The words we had written for each other the night before would be what stuck with me, along with the experiences we had shared over the course of five months. These were experiences that defied capture by the English language, and nods of understanding between pages were more common that day in the LBJ Room than the word goodbye.

I stepped out onto the Senate floor one last time before my family left the Capitol. I had spent countless hours in that chamber. During the past couple of weeks, it had been a favorite spot of mine in which to take a break from studying for final exams. I would just sit and think about how hard it would be to say goodbye to such a special place. My family waited for me in the Senate lobby as I took it all in for a couple more moments. I looked out over the 100 desks and up to the rostrum where the presiding officer sits. I looked down at the steps where the pages had bravely sat on September 12, 2001. I stood alone in a place where so many great statesmen had crafted the policies of a nation. It was a place that had hosted some of the greatest debates in our history and some of the most wonderful speeches.

I was at a loss for words, though. With a frog in my throat and water in my eyes, I nodded a goodbye to the home of the greatest legislative body in the world.

CHAPTER 17
2002 STATE OF THE UNION

I had a strange feeling while watching a new group of Senate pages welcome the President of the United States into the House chamber for the State of the Union address. I had been at home in South Dakota for just over a week when President Bush came to the Capitol for his first State of the Union since the terrorist attacks. I was a bit jealous that these pages would get to witness this speech during their first week on the job. A lot of the pages in my class wished that our term had lasted just a few more days, so we could have seen our President in action again.

My time as a page was up, though, and all I could do was take in the speech in front of my television. While it was strange to see the new pages in the back of the House chamber, it was stranger yet to be transitioning back into life away from the Capitol. I began classes at my regular high school back home, but there would be no more crack of dawn classes followed by a day of work on the Senate floor. I began to reconnect with my South Dakota friends in school, but there would be no more fun times hanging out with Senate page friends in Webster Hall. It was a difficult transition at times, and I learned quickly how much I would miss the Senate Page Program.

I was no longer a Senate page, but I was still an American. Every American was looking to the President on January 29, 2002, for a way forward in this war. My group of Senate pages had invested the whole of our energy in standing up to the terrorist attacks. Coming back to work on September 12th and persevering through the anthrax threat were not easy things to do, but we did them. At the same time, we understood that the war was not over. Our challenges as Senate pages had ended, but a generation's challenge was just beginning. Although I wished I could have been there in person, I sat down that evening in front of the television to see our President set the course for what would surely be a long struggle.

"As we gather tonight," President Bush began, "our nation is at war, our economy is in recession, and the civilized world faces unprecedented dangers. Yet the state of our Union has never been stronger." In a pre-9/11 world, it would have been hard to believe that the strongest moment for our country would be realized when such negative conditions as war and recession were prominent. We were coming out of a decade of peace and prosperity. Growing budget surpluses and a generally strong economy had been coupled with a sense that, with the peaceful bliss of the end of the Cold War, we no longer needed a strong military. Unfortunately, this was a false sense of security, and the terrorists had been plotting the entire time.

We had paid the price of complacency, but we would turn the tables on the terrorists quickly and show them that they had miscalculated when they thought of us as a paper tiger. "In four short months, our nation has comforted the victims, begun to rebuild New York and the Pentagon, rallied a great coalition, captured, arrested, and rid the world of thousands of terrorists, destroyed Afghanistan's terrorist training camps, saved a people from starvation, and freed a country from brutal oppression," Bush explained.

The military conflict in Afghanistan and the larger war on terror took center stage in this State of the Union address. Bush used some of the second half of his speech to discuss domestic issues, but even those comments were placed in the context of national security. The first half of the speech was a status report on how we were doing so far in this war and where this war would take us in the future.

Toward the beginning of the speech, the President welcomed two guests sitting in the gallery, Hamid Karzai and Sima Samar, who served as compelling symbols of the righteousness of our cause in Afghanistan. Karzai was the interim leader of Afghanistan at the time, and Samar was the new minister of Women's Affairs. Karzai would go on to be freely elected by the Afghan people to continue leading their liberated country. Samar's presence in the House chamber symbolized the transformational changes going on in a new Afghanistan that rejected the Taliban and accepted women in government.

After praising the Afghan leaders for the progress being made in the fledgling democracy, the commander in chief turned his attention to the credit due to the forces under his control. "When I called our troops into action, I did so with complete confidence in their courage and skill. And tonight, thanks to them, we are winning the War on Terror," Bush proclaimed to a roar of applause.

I think this assessment was correct. We were winning at this point. A lot of the credit for this should go to the "courage and skill" of our armed forces, but another reason we were winning was much simpler. The straightforward facts that we were willing to fight back against the terrorists, that we wanted to win, and that the consequences of complacency were still fresh in our minds provided the necessary criteria for America to be winning the war at this point.

For those who had clarity in January of 2002 and applauded Bush's speech but have grown weary of the daily costs of war, I point to a passage of that speech where our President explained the nature of this new war:

> Our cause is just, and it continues. Our discoveries in Afghanistan confirmed our worst fears, and showed us the true scope of the task ahead. We have seen the depth of our enemies' hatred in videos, where they laugh about the loss of innocent life. And the depth of their hatred is equaled by the madness of the destruction they design. We have found diagrams of American nuclear power plants and public water facilities, detailed instructions

*for making chemical weapons, surveillance maps of American
cities, and thorough descriptions of landmarks in America and
throughout the world. What we have found in Afghanistan con-
firms that, far from ending there, our war against terror is only
beginning.*

This warning from the past that this war would continue to be waged
beyond the borders of Afghanistan may not bring much comfort to someone who is tired of the war. But those who want to win can be comforted by
the fact that we are carrying out a winning strategy for the broader war.

"Our nation will continue to be steadfast and patient and persistent
in the pursuit of two great objectives," Bush explained. "First, we will
shut down terrorist camps, disrupt terrorist plans, and bring terrorists
to justice. And, second, we must prevent the terrorists and regimes who
seek chemical, biological or nuclear weapons from threatening the United
States and the world."

The second of these two objectives has proven to be the more contro-
versial, but the constant pursuit of both objectives is essential to showing
the terrorists that we are willing to fight, that we want to win, and that we
understand the costs of allowing them any breathing room. This is a war
that could eventually be waged with weapons of mass destruction (WMDs)
against our citizens. This means that a single day, a single event, could
bring the American death toll to the level of the entire Second World War.
The only difference would be that these casualties would be almost exclusively civilians instead of soldiers fighting in conventional war.

President Bush noted that the dangerous regimes which had sought
WMDs had been strangely quiet since the events of 9/11. They were trying
to be on their best behavior to avoid any scrutiny, I suppose, but our President understood the consequences of turning a blind eye. He spoke of
the atrocities of North Korea, Iran, and Iraq. Their people were innocent
victims of ruling elites that dictated their lives rather than daring to allow
them freedom. Each country either possessed, had previously possessed,
or was attempting to obtain WMDs.

President Bush would not let the leaders of these three countries off the hook. Instead, he pointed to the second objective in waging the broader war on terror by saying, "Our second goal is to prevent regimes that sponsor terror from threatening America or our friends and allies with weapons of mass destruction." After pointing out the problems posed by North Korea, Iran, and Iraq, Bush made a famous statement, "States like these, and their terrorist allies, constitute an axis of evil, arming to threaten the peace of the world." The willingness to call evil by its name harkens back to Reagan's leadership against the "evil empire" of the Soviet Union.

It is important to give the full sentence from the speech rather than only citing North Korea, Iran, and Iraq as the axis of evil. The reference to "states like these" would clearly include Syria in the club, and "their terrorist allies" brings Hamas, Hezbollah, and al-Qaeda into plain sight. At first glance this seems to make our war all the more difficult, and it begs the question, "Why take on Iraq first when we have all these other members in the 'axis of evil'?" Some have even argued that the use of the "axis of evil" phrase was misguided or, worse, a self-fulfilling prophecy. This view needs to be dismissed, though, because these states and terrorist groups were evil long before Bush labeled them as such. More importantly, a willingness to call a spade a spade is just as essential in fighting the War on Terror as the willingness to actively engage the enemy.

Bush used the word "evil" at another point in the speech in an even more revealing way when comparing our renewed will to defend freedom in the wake of 9/11 to the dashed expectations of our enemies. "During these last few months, I've been humbled and privileged to see the true character of this country in a time of testing," Bush said. "Our enemies believed America was weak and materialistic, that we would splinter in fear and selfishness. They were as wrong as they are evil."

Bush received applause for this use of the word evil, as well as for references to missile defense, to Guantanamo Bay detentions, and even a subtle reference to his willingness to use force preemptively. In a later political climate, Bush would have trouble getting the same applause for these ideas. Bush enjoyed an approval rating of around 80% at the time of the 2002 State of the Union address. Bush has since lost about half of that base of support, and it doesn't take a trained political scientist to boil the reason for this down to one word—Iraq.

Nonetheless, I will make two arguments to those who approved of the President back in January of 2002. First, I will make the case that Iraq was the logical point, the logical member of the axis of evil, with which to begin the expansion of the broader War on Terror. Second, I will argue that the accomplishments in Iraq and in the broader War on Terror since going into Iraq have been worth the costs.

Every argument making a case for a certain direction in the War on Terror links back to the Pearl Harbor-like events of September 11, 2001. President Bush made a reference to this important day in his first State of the Union after the attacks, and his statement provides the proper spring-board to make the case for going into Iraq. "In a single instant, we realized that this will be a decisive decade in the history of liberty, that we've been called to a unique role in human events. Rarely has the world faced a choice more clear or consequential," Bush said.

The clear choice behind which our nation was resolved was defending our freedoms and helping others taste freedom for themselves in Afghanistan. In the wake of 9/11, America and its President made the clear and consequential choice to confront evil head-on. Bush made reference to the decisive nature of the coming decade in the cause of liberty over terror. He had warned time and again that this would be a long struggle and a new kind of war. This does not mean that we should occasionally throw a dart at a map and attack a new country to keep the broader war going just for the sake of it. It does not even mean we should pick randomly from the list of the axis of evil and attack militarily.

A large part of confronting evil in a post-9/11 world was accomplished in this State of the Union just by naming names, but the heavy lifting remained. This question also remained: which evil regime should we confront first and most directly, considering that the confrontation could result in military action? Military action was not a complete necessity, but we had to continue to stand up against evil through diplomatic and economic means at the very least. The terrorists would only see weakness if we called the regime change in Afghanistan complete victory and went home.

Iran would have been one option. The Iranians have strong ties to terrorism, mainly through their support for Hezbollah. I know of no evidence linking the Iranians or Hezbollah directly to the 9/11 attacks, so citing only their other terror ties may have been a difficult case for going after Iran immediately after Afghanistan. Their creation of nuclear weapons was seen to be at least a handful of years away, and the diplomatic and economic sanctions would have to be at least attempted before any allies could be recruited into a war to oust the theocracy in Iran. The land mass of Iran is much bigger than Iraq, so one can imagine that the ensuing occupation would be at least as difficult as that of Iraq, if not more so.

North Korea needed to be dealt with as soon as possible, but it was a horse of a different color altogether. It was believed that North Korea already had nuclear weapons, so that created a strong military deterrent. This member of the axis of evil probably had the weakest ties to Islamic terrorism, so a shift to North Korea would have been odd. Also, those who are queasy about the losses in Iraq would not have wanted to try their luck in North Korea. Even without the possibility of a nuke hitting Tokyo or Seoul, the thought of the American and South Korean casualties created by a conventional attack would be enough to cause one to invest more faith in diplomacy.

The six-party talks hold the most hope for solving our problems with this member of the axis of evil. Bringing China, Russia, Japan, South Korea, and the U.S. to the table with North Korea could prove to be a great way to avoid the possibility of nuclear war in the region. North Korea is already isolated, so sanctions do little good, but China holds enough sway to bring Kim Jong-Il into line. The verdict back in 2002 must have been that diplomacy had a chance and the price of military action was too high.

Therefore, we are left with Iraq. Just because the other members of the axis of evil proved to be less-than-great candidates for the focused efforts of the American diplomatic, economic, and military might didn't necessarily mean that it was time to focus these energies on Iraq. It was the right time to take on Iraq, though. Saddam Hussein had had WMDs in the past, may have had them in 2002, and would most likely have pursued them further in the future. His connections to terror were less developed than Iran's, but he did give money to the families of Palestinian suicide bombers. He probably knew about the presence of al-Qaeda member Abu Musab al-Zarqawi in his country but did nothing about it. Saddam's biggest and clearest connection to terrorism was himself. He used chemical weapons on the Kurds in the north of Iraq. He brutally abused the Shia Muslims who accounted for a majority of the population in his country.

The main reason Iraq stood out on the list of the axis of evil was the country's direct history with the U.S. Saddam's 1990 invasion of Kuwait had resulted in nearly 300 deaths of American troops trying to liberate Kuwait. Saddam had intentions of dominating his region by controlling oil and deterring military opposition by obtaining WMDs. The Gulf War did not go to Baghdad, though, and Saddam was left in power. A sanctions regime had been put in place and weapons inspectors had largely dismantled the weapons program in Iraq. Saddam seemed somewhat contained, but he kicked out the weapons inspectors in the latter half of the Clinton administration. President Clinton and the U.S. Congress seemed ready to take action against Saddam, but nothing major came of it. The United Nations continued to condemn Saddam over his weapons and tried to enforce an abysmally corrupt sanctions regime known as Oil for Food. Without strong American diplomacy against Iraq, the UN might have discarded the sanctions completely, and Saddam would have been able to do as he pleased.

Now, we fast forward through 9/11 and on to the State of the Union address in January 2002. With all of this history in play, the President rightfully condemned Iraq as an evil regime that should be confronted. It follows that it was completely rational for the President to go to the UN a year after the 9/11 attacks and demand that attention be given to the problem of Saddam and Iraq. The world would try diplomacy one more time, or Saddam would famously face "serious consequences." With the

American military built up in the Gulf, it was not hard to decipher what serious consequences meant to the Americans, British, Australians, and Poles, among others in the "coalition of the willing."

The military action in Iraq ended up being a war of choice—Saddam's choice. He chose not to meet the demands of the UN Security Council. There was new backing and new credibility in the world system, though. President Bush meant what he said, and he carried it out to create a democracy in Iraq. If you can see that confronting Iraq as a member of the axis of evil was the right thing to do, you should agree that it was right to go to the UN in 2002. If you think it was a just decision for Bush to confront Iraq on a world stage at the UN a year after the attacks of 9/11, you should also realize the ensuing war was just as well.

As I write these words, American resolve is being tested in Iraq. The terrorists are challenging our principles of being willing to fight, wanting to win, and understanding the costs of complacency. Regardless of your opinion on what America should have done after Afghanistan, the truth of the matter is that we are invested in Iraq now. Victory is the only exit strategy, and fighting half-way does no good for America's security or the Iraqi people's future.

My second argument is that the benefits of this war have been worth the fighting (and dying) for. I will argue this with a simple hypothetical scenario that requires you to place yourself back in time to January 2002. Imagine that President Bush had announced in his State of the Union address that because of the 9/11 attacks America would prosecute a vigorous and broad War on Terror to protect the homeland from another attack, especially one involving WMDs. Imagine that Bush had said that we would liberate the countries of Afghanistan and Iraq from brutal regimes with a loss of American life approximately equal to the 3,000 lives lost on 9/11 spread out over the course of the next five years. These countries would have free elections to form constitutions and governments. Imagine that Bush had then guaranteed that because we fought the terrorists abroad there would be no attacks on the homeland for at least five years. Bush would have explained that the war would be expensive in dollars, but the

economy would pull out of its recession in 2003 and run at near full em-
ployment.

Can you imagine the reaction to these public statements? I can hear
the talking heads and pundits on television after the address finished. "It
was totally irresponsible for the President to guarantee such *success* in
defending the homeland at the infant stages of this war on terror," one
commentator would assert.

"He's declaring a *major achievement* before we've even begun to
fight," another broadcaster would complain.

"The President needs to wake up and understand that 3,000 deaths
would hardly get us to Baghdad, let alone turn the operation into a *victory* like a functioning democracy as he predicts," another analyst would
opine.

Of course, they would all be correct that such public predictions from
the crystal ball would be irresponsible, but any rational person in January
of 2002 would have agreed that this hypothetical future scenario would be
defined as success, victory, or a major achievement at the time, completely
worth the cost of 3,000 soldiers, especially in the context of preventing
attacks at home. Of course, every lost soldier is an enormous cost, and
the many wounded for every death is an important consideration. Still, it
is interesting to see the difference in the public's resolved reaction to the
3,000 deaths that started the War on Terror compared with the apprehension over the 3,000 deaths out of a volunteer military of heroes who
have liberated 50 million people and prevented attacks on their homeland
through their line of work.

The blame for these casualties can be laid at the doorstep (or spider
hole) of one man. Saddam decided to ignore the terms of the end of the
Gulf War and pursue weapons, or at least give the world reason to think he
had something to hide. And in this post-9/11 atmosphere, the burden of
proof was on Saddam. Clearly, the best rationale for this war is that it is a
necessary extension of the first Gulf War, and enforcing the terms of that
war is essential to honor those who died liberating Kuwait and to maintain
our credibility in confronting evil. In October of 2002, when this version

of history was understood, the U.S. Senate endorsed the military option in Iraq with a 77-23 vote. Sadly, it now takes a profile in courage to stay true to one's original support for this extension of the first Gulf War, as demonstrated by Senator Joe Lieberman.

Our troubles in Iraq continue, but we should not be quick to shrug off the great accomplishments. Free elections have created a constitution and a representative government. The Iraqis are standing up to defend their own country and joining the police and military forces. The Kurdish area in the north and the Shia area in the south have been largely pacified and turned over to Iraqi control.

Baghdad remains the major issue that just won't go away. It reminds me of a time when another city was written off as a haven for crime, vice, and corruption. The situation was worsened further by a defeatist attitude. New York City needed a leader like Mayor Rudy Giuliani who was willing to be creative, to invest the resources, and to ignore the initial criticism in order to transform the city into the greatest in the world. The real message is that Americans can take comfort in all the good we are doing in the world and in those leaders who do exhibit profiles in courage.

Regardless, just imagine that the President could have told you of these future outcomes privately instead of in an irresponsible public forum. All the costs would now be paid up front in your mind. You wouldn't have to learn about a couple of U.S. servicemen dying each day for five years on the news. You would have what is called perspective. You would see the big picture. The media can only give it to you one day at a time, but you have the power to take yourself back and listen to the final passage of President Bush's remarks in his 2002 State of the Union and know exactly how the War on Terror has progressed.

Bush finished his speech by declaring, "Steadfast in our purpose, we now press on. We have known freedom's price. We have shown freedom's power. And in this great conflict, my fellow Americans, we will see freedom's victory."

Chapter 18
Life after DC

M y life settled down quite a bit after the incredible five months spent in Washington, D.C. I continued to face my share of challenges, though. Finishing high school could have been a breeze, but I chose to seek out leadership positions and apply to my dream school, the University of Notre Dame. Once at Notre Dame, it would have been easy to choose a simple life of academics combined with some football watching, but I worked hard to find a way to serve my country further though the Air Force ROTC program. Difficulties and setbacks along the way have turned out to be blessings that have confirmed further that God has a plan for me.

In the spring of 2002, I went to a political rally in Sioux Falls, South Dakota, that President Bush attended. He had an inspiring message that made me once again nostalgic for my days in Washington as a U.S. Senate page. He said something that inspired me to do more than think back in time, though. Bush had a forward-looking message of optimism and hope in fighting the world's evils. He has been a President who has taken a lot of heat for oversimplifying complex issues, but on this count his simplicity was as powerful as it was correct. He said, "The best way to fight evil is to do good."

I remember that day in the Sioux Falls Arena very well. I remember my dad and I being moved nearly to tears when the President mentioned the strength of his resolve to protect the homeland. It touched both of our hearts and stirred many of the emotions I had experienced back in the fall of 2001. That quote inspired me to do more to fight this evil in our world, even if what I would do would only contribute a small good. When I got back to school, I sought out the student council advisor and asked how to get involved and run for office.

I soon became baffled by the level of apathy in student government and by the indifference that led to ineffectiveness. I was elected to be one of six representatives for the senior class on the student council, but only five candidates even came forward with the interest to run. Therefore, we did not even have an assembly to give our speeches to our fellow students, and our first item of business was selecting a sixth member. Coming from an experience with the greatest legislative body in the world to this student council was a disillusioning experience to say the least.

I attacked the problems in the system as a maverick reformer in the mold of the feisty Senator McCain, but the power of the status quo made me hit a wall quickly. Instead of helping garner support for common-sense reform to make student government relevant in my high school, the other students on the council saw no reason to change a system that left them in control with no interest from the student body to challenge them. It was a frustrating time for me, but I learned an important lesson about entrenched bureaucracies: sometimes it is better to achieve incremental change and win over more allies before attempting fundamental change. Unfortunately, I had only one year to be a council member. Nevertheless, I carry no shame that my greatest achievement in the world of student government came as vice president of the Senate Page Student Council in crafting the resolution honoring Lieutenant Colonel Birdwell.

I did find some success in another venture during my senior year. I was elected president of my high school's chapter of National Honor Society (NHS). It was in this role that I had the most opportunities to follow Bush's advice of fighting evil by doing good for others. I helped organize some community service events and cheered on other students who did other independent forms of service. All members had to complete 40 hours of service to graduate with the NHS distinction, and I was proud to be one of those members, let alone the leader of the chapter.

I learned some great life lessons from these two positions in my senior year, and I am sure they looked great on my college applications. When it came time to write my personal statement to my dream school, however, only one story would suffice. It was my first attempt at expressing my Senate page experience through writing, and to this day I think it made all the difference.

My road to South Bend, Indiana, did not run smooth. After I tried to apply in an early admission format, Notre Dame deferred me into the regular pool of applicants. Notre Dame then gave me a further scare by placing me on the waiting list in April of 2003. While I was also excited about the possibility of following in the footsteps of some great South Dakotans by becoming a Jackrabbit at South Dakota State University in my hometown of Brookings, Notre Dame remained my first choice if only I could get in off that waiting list. My parents were especially excited about SDSU and their offer to me of a nearly free education, but each of us still prayed for good news from the Fighting Irish.

I became resigned to the fact that I would graduate from high school in late May of 2003 without knowing for sure which college I would be attending. It was a frustrating feeling, but I learned to treat it as yet another test. I knew God had the right answer, and if I was meant to get into Notre Dame, it would happen. A couple of weeks before my high school graduation, a phone call came that would determine where I would spend the next four years of my life. My mom handed me the phone with a certain level of giddiness, knowing that it had to be good news, and she was right. I quickly accepted the offer to be part of Notre Dame's class of 2007. Not only did I get to graduate with the knowledge of where I was going, but I also had the opportunity to address my high school class as a future Golden Domer. I will share more about my graduation speech at the end of this chapter.

Getting accepted to my dream school did not necessarily mean a fairy tale ending. There would still be challenges ahead and new lessons to learn. I knew Notre Dame would be a challenging school academically, but I had survived the surroundings of the Senate Page School. My fellow pages had been smart enough to get into world-class institutions like Princeton, Georgetown, Duke, Emory, the University of Pennsylvania, and the University of North Carolina, to name a few. I had fared pretty well in one semester of competing with top-notch kids like these, and I had made it into a top-25 institution myself.

College was not like high school, though. I couldn't just skate by on natural ability and expect to be among the top students in every class. I learned quickly that straight A's every semester were not in the cards at Notre Dame quite like they had been in high school. In a couple of cases during my career at Notre Dame, I had to work very hard to avoid getting a "C" for a final grade in a class. Who knew economics could be made so difficult? Anyway, I ended up being prouder of my 3.7 GPA at Notre Dame than of my 4.0 in high school because college was a whole different world.

It was an adjustment that had to be made by most of my classmates. Many of them had never received a "B" in their lives before college, but some got a rude awakening with low grades on their first college papers or tests. Some would freak out, and some would take it in stride, but everyone adjusted eventually. I had to realize that, in any given classroom, I was in the middle of the pack, rather than at the top of the heap like in high school. I still had to enter that classroom with the confidence that I could get a top grade if I worked hard enough, though. It took this balance in attitude of confidence and modesty to succeed at such a high-caliber school.

Notre Dame was a fun atmosphere because I was surrounded by so many intelligent kids who could carry on intelligent conversations about a variety of topics. I could talk with the guys in my dorm about politics or finances. I could talk with friends about philosophy and theology. And I could talk with almost anyone about Notre Dame football!

Academics were tough at Notre Dame during my first two years, but watching the football team was even harder! The team had a great year when I was a senior in high school but lost the magic during my freshman and sophomore years of college. Those were the last two years of Coach Ty Willingham, and then the era of Charlie Weis began. Weis definitely has the storied football program back on the right track, and this provided a lot more fun for me during my last two football seasons as a student.

The first two seasons were hard to watch because I had been a Notre Dame football fan since the fourth grade. That year in school, my teacher was 100 percent Irish and taught me about Irish culture. I took to it quickly because my Grandma Kippley had been 100 percent Irish as well, which left me with a quarter Irish blood. It was about this same time in the early 1990s that I started watching the football games with my dad, and I loved cheering for the team with the golden helmets. Seeing the movie *Rudy* then compounded all these elements into a strong desire to attend the school. Plenty of the students at Notre Dame had had their own *Rudy* experiences; seeing the movie just made them fall in love with the idea of Notre Dame and realize it is a special place (and as a consequence, the admissions people get sick of reading stories about the movie in applicants' personal statements!).

I was not a happy person after witnessing a loss at Notre Dame Stadium. Unfortunately, this meant I was not a happy person very often when Willingham was doing the coaching. I often lamented that they shouldn't make us do our homework for the rest of the weekend if we suffered a loss on Saturday. Mediocre records of 5-7 and 6-6 led to Willingham's dismissal and the eventual hiring of Weis from his spot as the offensive coordinator with the New England Patriots.

Weis was an alumnus of Notre Dame and understood that the program needed to start its winning ways again. He made the rounds to talk with students about the football program, and when he came to my dorm, I was excited for the chance to hear him speak. He had a simple attitude and a competitive drive that allowed him to make bold statements. I remember that he told us that he planned on winning every game that first year. He didn't guarantee that he would win them all, but he was committing himself to doing everything he could to win each game. The Irish would go on to lose only three games that season and win nine. The spirit of the team had noticeably changed as well. Even in the three losses, Weis was playing to win rather than just trying to keep the score respectable.

This is an important attitude that is relevant to other areas of life. In some things, going for decisive victory is the only option, and there is no room for a defeatist attitude or half-measures. I heard a comment around campus early on in Weis's coaching days that struck me as funny and meaningful. Someone said that it is frustrating, with all the trouble in the world with terrorism, economic problems, and social problems, that the smartest man in the world is only coaching football. Weis is considered an offensive genius when it comes to football, but of course he is just a football coach. His outlook on how to approach the game can serve us well as we take on the tasks of this generation, though. In fighting the War on Terror, winning is our only option, and we must fight every battle with a plan to win decisively. We won't necessarily win every engagement, military or otherwise, but the attitude, the morale, and the spirit will carry us to an eventual victory against an enemy that can only offer oppression and despair. Sometimes it takes a simple philosophy from a sports figure to give us the best guidance our generation can get on what to do about terrorism: Win!

While the academics at Notre Dame proved challenging and the first two seasons of football were disappointing, my toughest trial came when I was dismissed from the Air Force ROTC program for medical reasons. My first thoughts toward the idea of serving in the military came after meeting Lieutenant Colonel Birdwell in 2001. I wanted to continue to serve my country in some manner after proudly serving the U.S. Senate as a page, and the military proved to be a great fit for me. I chose the ROTC program because it would allow me to learn a lot of leadership skills, as well as a commission as an officer after finishing college. The Air Force offered me a scholarship that would help with the tremendous cost of a private school education and turn a dream school into a financial possibility. After visiting with the officers assigned to Notre Dame's detachment, I determined that the Air Force seemed like a good fit for me, and I soon found myself looking forward to at least a few years in the military as an intelligence officer or an attorney.

I started out strong as a first-year Air Force cadet at Notre Dame. I maintained a high enough GPA in my first year of school to earn an increase in my scholarship. I worked hard to improve my physical fitness level and leadership ability. As a scholarship cadet, I went to Minot (North Dakota) Air Force Base for some training the summer after my freshman year. Through my position on the Honor Guard, I had the chance to watch my first Irish football game as a student from the field. If you could have told the fourth-grade version of me that I'd be on Notre Dame's football field in uniform during my freshman year, I am sure I would have been ecstatic at the thought of playing football for the Irish. This uniform was an Air Force uniform, but I was just as ecstatic.

Chills ran down my spine as I walked through the tunnel and out on the field. My job that day was to support the color guard by helping uncase their flags as they prepared to march out onto the field for the National Anthem. We remained on the field for the rest of the game as the Irish went on to defeat Washington State by a field goal. In the fall of my sophomore year, I got the chance to be a member of the color guard detail itself and march on the field for the Purdue game. Later in the fall of 2004, I was offered the position as Honor Guard commander for the spring semester. It was exactly what I wanted to do because I enjoyed honoring the flag and the traditions of our armed forces. God had a different plan for me, though.

That same season, I was diagnosed with Crohn's Disease, a chronic gastrointestinal problem. When I reported this fact to the colonel at Notre Dame, he informed me that the chronic nature of the disease would result in a medical disqualification from the ROTC program. Luckily, my case of Crohn's has been mild and stable, so my health has not really suffered. The only change in my day-to-day life has involved taking a couple of pills, so I thank God that the health situation is not as bad as it could have been.

Obviously, this would also result in the end of my scholarship, placing a new hardship on my family. Not only did I have to find a new plan for a career upon graduation, but I also had to find a way to afford a Notre Dame education. My first instinct was to fight the Air Force's decision. I got a second opinion from another doctor, to no avail. I even pulled out the big guns and called Senator Daschle's office. The Senator's staff was very helpful in trying to find some way for me to remain in the military, but no loopholes could be found. The diagnosis was what it was, so it did not matter that my case was only a mild one.

For a few days, I had to really consider the possibility of leaving Notre Dame and returning home to a state school in South Dakota. The loss of the scholarship meant that my family and I would have to carry the full burden of the $20,000-per-semester bill from Notre Dame for four more semesters. I was put into a situation where it would have been easy and understandable to retreat. I had been in a similar situation before, though, and there would be no retreating this time either. After giving due consideration to the financial situation, my family and I decided to do whatever it would take to make sure I could finish my degree at Notre Dame. At school I had the support of some close friends whose care for me could only be matched by my old Senate page friends and my family. I put myself on a fast track to graduate one semester early to save money, and I was still able to major in both political science and economics.

My military career had been cut short by circumstances out of my control, but the situation gave me yet another opportunity to make the most out of a difficult situation. I renewed my faith in the idea that when one door closes, another one will open. A multitude of other possibilities presented themselves once the strict training requirements of the Air Force were taken off of my schedule. My summers would no longer be taken up by military training at Air Force bases. I could take this extra time and put it toward other projects like government internships and writing this book.

There were definitely moments of doubt while I went through this process of leaving the Air Force. There were definitely worries about how it would all work out, but it was invaluable for me to be able to look back to my Senate page experience and rely on the faith that a higher power was looking out for me. There have been challenges in my life thus far, there will be more challenges to come, and I wouldn't have it any other way.

Some adversity will come in the common course of daily life, and some trials will be on a scale larger than any one of our lives alone. The War on Terror is such a trial. Like 9/11, some moments come along that change the world forever and clarify the role a generation must play in history. The task at hand is so large and global in scope that no individual can have all the answers or solve all the problems. It is a challenge that will bring out the best in each of us as we prove that doing good and spreading freedom's promise can defeat any evil. Our resolve, our willingness to sacrifice, and our desire to win will be tested. This is truly a generation's challenge.

While I can no longer join in this important battle for freedom as a member of the U.S. military, I can share my perspective through the power of words. I have already shared with you some great quotations of U.S. Senators in the aftermath of 9/11 to show what a sense of purpose and a feeling of unity in the U.S Congress can sound like. I hope that you refer to President Bush's speech from September 20, 2001, or his 2002 State of the Union address whenever you feel yourself losing that sense of purpose. If none of these elected leaders can provide the right words for you in your quest for a reason for hope and optimism as we fight this war, I hope that some of my own words from a speech can ring clear as a resolved message from one proud member of this embattled generation.

I began to articulate my ideas on the broad scope of what the War on Terror means about a year after leaving the Senate page program. I began to put my thoughts into writing as I learned that I would have the opportunity to address my fellow high school students at our graduation ceremony in May of 2003. This speech, along with my Senate page experience, became the template for this book, and I feel it is important to share the text of that speech with you.

Today is a day when we hold tight to memories of the past, yet we will soon move forward to take on the future and make our mark in this world. Before our generation can take a place in history, we must remember those who have come before us.

For their sacrifices and achievements, our grandparents have been dubbed the "Greatest Generation." And rightly so. The work ethic to rise out of the Great Depression, the strength of mind and body to win World War II, and the determination to stand up against communism embodied this "Greatest Generation."

The next generation, our parents' generation, saw to it that walls were brought down here at home—and in Berlin. They were part of our Brookings education system as teachers, fans, and loving supporters through thick and thin. But what I guess I'm trying to say is that we have something to thank all of them for even before they give us graduation gifts!

Yes, we all have great things to remember from our K-12 years, and yes, we have learned many things along the way. But it is now more important for our class to look back on those things that we—our class, our generation—must never forget.

In May 2001, President Bush gave the commencement speech at his alma mater, Yale University. He said, "When I left here, I didn't have much in the way of a life plan. I knew some people who thought they did. But it turned out that we were all in for ups and downs, most of them unexpected. Life takes its own turns, makes its own demands, and writes its own story, and along the way we start to realize we are not the author."

He said this to a graduating group like ours not knowing that, months later, life would take a sudden turn and make an important demand. A higher power than either you or I composed a huge task for us on September 11, 2001. We did not ask for a war on terror to be placed on our shoulders, but it is a task that we must complete for the sake of future generations. We will fight this evil by doing good for others and ensuring that our freedoms created centuries ago will be preserved for centuries to come. We will remember the actions of those who came before us.

And finally, we will move forward in the spirit of the heroic words of Todd Beamer, who helped bring down the hijacked plane in Pennsylvania before it could take the lives of others. Class of 2003, "Let's Roll!"

The "lives of others" that I referred to at the end of this speech included my friends and coworkers in the Capitol. These were the folks that I grew to love over the course of five months of serving the U.S. Senate. These were real people, not abstract concepts. No politician needs to remind us of the value of those people in our lives. No words of inspiration are as powerful as the thought of doing whatever is necessary to defend those we love. In the end, Americans' resolve will hold strong because an unwavering resolve is exactly what is required to successfully defend our loved ones in this kind of war.

Each anniversary of the 9/11 attacks provides an opportunity for Americans as individuals and as a united country to remember the terrorists' attack on our sacred symbols and our fellow citizens. For some of us, those memories are with us every day, but when that date arrives on the calendar each year, all of us take notice and remember how real people became heroes in order to save lives and defend our love for liberty.

CHAPTER 19
FIVE ANNIVERSARIES OF 9/11

The rolling hills of southwestern Pennsylvania looked amazing on the chilly morning of September 11, 2006. Five years earlier a beautiful day had been shattered by a commercial aircraft striking a field near Shanksville. This day brought overcast skies and a few sprinkles of rain, as well as hundreds of people, to the hallowed ground that was this field in rural Pennsylvania. My friend John Henderson and I were two of the many Americans who came to the temporary memorial for the Flight 93 passengers exactly five years after their heroism had saved countless lives in Washington, D.C.

I had been planning this trip throughout the summer of 2006, and I was excited when my friend John decided to join me. John served in Air Force ROTC with me at the Notre Dame detachment. By the time of our trip to Shanksville, both of us were out of the ROTC program, so we were seeking new ways to serve our country. John was one of a few close friends who helped me through my difficult ordeal of being medically disqualified from the ROTC program. He also knew the story of my service as a U.S. Senate page in the fall of 2001 and understood the meaning of the Shanksville site to me.

We drove from South Bend, Indiana to Somerset, Pennsylvania on Sunday, September 10th, and stayed the night in a hotel just 30 minutes away from the memorial. The drive was somewhere between six and seven hours. It provided plenty of time for John and me to talk politics and

Notre Dame football and share stories of our ROTC days. It also provided plenty of time to reflect on the heroism displayed on Flight 93 and to look back on the commemoration of past anniversaries of the terrorist attacks.

I had some special moments on each anniversary of the attacks leading up to the fifth anniversary ceremony at the Flight 93 memorial. These days were times of reflection and growth. These days were times of renewed sorrow and anger, but they were also celebrations of courage and lives saved. Each anniversary lent itself to a combination of looking back to the events of that day and looking forward to securing a future in which it never happens again.

On the first anniversary of the attacks, I was back at my high school in South Dakota. I remember sitting in my journalism classroom that morning and watching a ceremony going on in New York City on the television. They were reading the names of those who had lost their lives a year earlier. I sat quietly in my desk, watched some of the coverage on the news, and listened to others in my class recount their experiences from the day of the attacks.

A few kids in the back of the room commented on where they were when they found out about the World Trade Center being hit. All of their stories were very similar, of course, because it had been a Tuesday morning, and they were all in one classroom or another inside the school when the news came. All of their stories were important, though. For each of them, it would be a moment they remembered forever.

Listening to these stories helped me realize that everyone in my generation was having these types of conversations on that day. They were asking each other how they found out the terrible news, where they were, and how they felt Most would have very simple answers of being in a classroom and seeing it on television or having a teacher inform them, but these simple moments would be seared in their minds forever. One didn't need to be in New York or Washington to be deeply affected by that day; one only needed to have a heart.

My classmates had been separated by hundreds of miles from the areas attacked, but the power of the media brought the images into South

Dakota classrooms within minutes. They would never understand completely what it was like to be in one of the targets of the day, but their conversations that morning led me to believe that they would never forget such a significant moment for our generation. I will never fully understand what it would have been like to be trapped in a tower in New York or to suffer burns in the Pentagon blaze, but I will never forget that the passengers of Flight 93 saved me and others in the Capitol from gaining that horrible understanding.

I continued to sit at the front of the classroom as the class period drifted along. I pretended to watch the news, but in reality, I was just thinking about the friends I had made in the fall of 2001 and the experiences we went through during that dreadful day and the weeks that came after it. I avoided the conversation in the back of the journalism classroom that day, so I could keep to my own thoughts. I also didn't want to dominate the other students' conversation about their experiences with the tale of my own crazy adventure in Washington.

The emotions were too strong that day to tell my own story well, anyway. It was the first time that the events of that day had been placed so squarely in the public mind since I had left the page program. It was the first time that I was confronted with the date that will live in infamy without my page family to stand alongside me. We were all back in our hometowns across this great nation. E-mails poured in throughout that month of September 2002 from my fellow Senate pages, and I talked to a few of them by phone on the 11th.

The comment would come up now and again that the first anniversary of the attacks confirmed Mrs. Owens's statement to us that we couldn't go home. The conversations that surrounded the first anniversary in our hometowns were so different from our experiences. We confided in one another about how we were doing one year after the attacks because it was hard to explain our feelings to someone who hadn't been with us through it all. We remembered our evacuation to Maryland and our determination to make the best of a difficult situation. We shared our pride in going back to work the next day and realized how much each of us had grown up during the one-year span of September 2001 to September 2002.

The first anniversary was an important milestone for me personally. I had been removed from the hustle and bustle of the Washington atmosphere for about eight months. The time had given me a chance to catch my breath and look back on all that had occurred while I was a Senate page. I was able to sit down on that day and really begin to grieve what had happened a year ago. I finally had the time to read Lisa Beamer's book and gain a greater understanding of the heroes on Flight 93. While we were pages, we didn't have much time to think about all these things, and it was easier not to think about them too hard.

It took a year for it all to settle in and gain its full effect. That effect was clear the entire time, though. We were a nation at war. We were a nation where average people would run into burning buildings to save others that they had never met. We were a nation that would strive to get over its wounds as Lieutenant Colonel Birdwell had gotten over his own wounds—through faith in a higher power, courage, and determination. We were a nation where 40 strangers could join forces to thwart the terrorists from success with a fourth plane. We were a nation where every citizen felt the pain of New York and Washington regardless of their distance from the crash sites. We were a nation united in the ideas of freedom and democracy over terror and totalitarianism. My generation was a generation willing to fight evil because of all that was good about this nation.

That first anniversary and all the personal development I had experienced in coming to terms with all my page class had been through went a long way. It would be four more years before I would visit the sacred ground near Shanksville, and it would turn out that I needed that much more time to be ready for the power of that simple memorial. Each of the intervening anniversaries would carry its own power, though, and I remember those days with the same vividness that others may remember the original 9/11 back in 2001.

The second anniversary came in 2003, and this would be the first 9/11 on which I had neither my own family nor my Senate page family with me.

I was a freshman at Notre Dame about halfway in between South Dakota and Washington, D.C. It was fairly early in the school year, so I was just getting to know my roommates and the other cadets in ROTC with me. I hadn't really told these new friends about my personal experiences in relation to the 9/11 attacks. I wouldn't completely be going it alone on this anniversary, though, because I carried a copy of Lisa Beamer's book with me that day.

The morning of the 11th included a military ceremony at which I stood in formation with my fellow Air Force cadets next to the Navy midshipmen and Army cadets. The ceremony was quite solemn, but it conveyed the optimistic message that our military could do its part to prevent these terrorist events from occurring again. The ceremony took place in between the library and Notre Dame Stadium. While listening to the speakers, all the cadets and midshipmen faced the library with its mural of "Touchdown Jesus." I couldn't help but take in this beautiful artwork and thank God for the opportunities that lay before me at such a wonderful school and for the heroes of 9/11 who had saved so many lives, possibly including my own.

After being dismissed from the ceremony, I headed back to my dorm and changed into civilian clothes. I lay in my bed for a while reading *Let's Roll!* About halfway through the story of Todd Beamer and Flight 93, I went out for some fresh air and a walk around the lakes. After walking around one of the lakes on the campus of Notre Dame, I stopped at the grotto to say a prayer and light a candle. It was one of my first experiences at the grotto as a student, and I couldn't think of a better reason to be there. After kneeling in front of the grotto, feeling thankful I had brought some tissues, I retreated to a bench 25 yards away facing the grotto. I read the heart-wrenching parts of Lisa's book and cried for a while.

I took a deep breath and looked around a little bit. God came through again in the beauty of nature. The walk around the lake behind me had been wonderful. The trees gave their first hints of changing color for the autumn season. I stared into the flame of the candle I had lit. It sat on the first rack of candles, zero rows across, and seven rows up—107. I had lit it with a prayer for my fellow Senate pages who had worked with me in the

107th Congress. The light shone alongside many others lit by students that day, candles lit by a generation that will never forget what had happened only two years earlier.

The third anniversary came and went in much the same way that the second had. The only two differences were that I was a sophomore and that it was a football Saturday at Notre Dame. The campus turned into a tourist site, with over 80,000 fans roaming the area in hopes of an Irish victory over Michigan.

I participated in my last 9/11 ceremony as an Air Force cadet that morning and headed to the grotto with my favorite book in hand. As I re-read a few of my favorite sections of Lisa's book, thousands of people came through the grotto area wearing Notre Dame and Michigan apparel. They knelt down in front of the grotto after lighting a candle to pray. I can tell you from personal experience that most prayers in that grotto on football Saturdays are for a solid win in Notre Dame Stadium that afternoon, but I like to think it was a bit different on September 11, 2004. Three years later, the loss of life and the great heroism of that day were still part of the American psyche, and even the avid football fans must have taken a moment at the beautiful grotto to reflect on the terrorist attack.

I read my book and cried my tears, quite oblivious to the crowds around me. I would join them as a part of the Notre Dame family when we got into the stadium, but I needed these few moments to myself. That morning I had woken up with the words "Let's roll!" echoing through my mind, as I start every day, but this time I definitely felt a presence. There is something magical about a home football weekend at Notre Dame that can't be explained. With that feeling and the feelings that came with the third anniversary of 9/11, I wasn't surprised to sense the presence of higher power that day. I prayed that Todd's heroic spirit would be with me that day, and with our football team, if we had any chance of beating Michigan!

Notre Dame would go on to beat the Wolverines 28-20 with a magical atmosphere pulsing through the stadium. It was a beautiful day for football, with just a few white, puffy clouds in the sky. I remember looking up to that sky after a key play had gone Notre Dame's way and smiling. I knew a great American hero was smiling back that day.

The fourth anniversary came in 2005 as I entered my junior year at Notre Dame. I went to the ceremony on campus as a civilian to listen to the speakers and support my girlfriend, Amanda Hettler, who was a second-year cadet at the Air Force detachment. This anniversary fell on a Sunday, so Amanda and I went to Catholic Mass in the Basilica on campus after the ceremony. It was a great feeling to have someone at my side on a difficult day for me.

I had met Amanda through the ROTC program, and we started dating in January of 2005. She was such a fun-loving person with such a wonderful smile that I couldn't pass her up. She had been there along with my friend John when I struggled through the process of being diagnosed with Crohn's Disease and the subsequent dismissal from the Air Force. Her attitude and smile reminded me of my great friend Jen Cohen from my days as a Senate page. Her strength of character and faith reminded me of Lisa Beamer. As we sat together listening to the homily by Fr. Richard Warner, I knew that I was blessed to have Amanda as a girlfriend.

I had learned many things and been blessed with many gifts in my short time on this earth thus far, but there was one thing I still had to do. It took about five years of preparation for my visit to rural Pennsylvania. I am glad I waited that long, because it would have been hard to take it all in when just one or two years had elapsed since the terrorist attacks. I had gained quite a bit of perspective after five years, but I did not want to wait any longer before paying my respects at the crash site of Flight 93.

On the morning of the fifth anniversary, John and I followed the directions of some locals in Somerset, Pennsylvania. We drove through the tiny town of Shanksville and followed the signs to the memorial from there. The state police were out directing the traffic toward the site of the temporary memorial. We made our way down a gravel path until a policeman directed us into a field to our left. This field would serve as the parking lot for hundreds of vehicles, while the field on the right served as a sacred cemetery for the fallen heroes in the first battle of the War on Terror.

After parking the car, we headed back to that gravel road. The path continued on down a hill and to the right, where a large tent was set up for the ceremony. Someone informed us that we could walk down to the ceremony or wait for a shuttle. We nodded our understanding but only looked straight ahead to the other side of the road. The small, temporary memorial was set up about 100 yards away, and another 500 yards beyond the memorial was the crash site itself, denoted only by an American flag and a small fence around its perimeter.

We headed toward the temporary memorial, which was essentially a tall fence decorated with patriotic messages left behind by past visitors. John and I took some pictures of the wall and the accompanying plaque with a list of all the passengers' names. Plenty of media personnel were there on that day, too, taking pictures of anything and everything. It was frustrating to see a dozen photographers swarm around a kid as he placed something at the memorial. I later found out that the child was the son of one of the pilots on board. On one hand, it seemed like the media was butting in on a lot of personal moments on hallowed ground, but on the other hand, some of these emotional moments need to be captured by the power of photography to remind the world of what happened that day.

There wasn't much more to look at or take pictures of at this memorial. It was beautiful in its simplicity. All of the surrounding fields in this area of rural Pennsylvania looked about the same, but this was *the one*. I had seen the images of this field on television on the day of the attacks, and I had seen pictures in the five intervening years since the crash, but being there in person was something else altogether. I looked out and reflected on the importance of this crash site being in this field rather than at its intended target in Washington.

My experience in the Capitol that day led to this otherwise random field in Pennsylvania holding a strong calling. Five years after the other passengers answered Todd Beamer's call of "Let's roll," I answered the call of this sacred ground to pay the respects I had owed for quite some time. I reflected on all the time that had passed since these passengers made the ultimate sacrifice. All the great things that had happened to me, some of which I have shared in the preceding pages, could not be taken for granted. A higher power with infinite wisdom let the passengers of Flight 93 bring that plane down in that field, and seeing that field for myself gave me the final closure that I needed.

It had been a five-year grieving process with plenty of emotions running through my body, yet five quiet minutes at this field near Shanksville had finally brought a sense of closure. I still have moments of sadness and anger when thinking of that terrible day in my second week as a Senate page, as most people do. That day in Shanksville was important, though, because it allowed me to pay my respects properly to those who died there and move forward in accomplishing the mission that they started.

After these special moments gazing out at the field of the crash site from the hilltop of the temporary memorial, I turned to John and said that I was ready to head down to the ceremony. We walked the path instead of taking the shuttle and soon reached the large white tent. Only special guests and family members of the Flight 93 passengers were allowed in the tent, so John and I had to stand behind a small fence. It was only at this point that we realized that we were freezing! The simple power of the place had made us disregard the low temperatures during that early morning for over a half hour. John went back up the hill to my car to grab our sweatshirts. We were not pleased with the meteorologists who had predicted a high of 72 degrees with no warning that it would only be in the high 40s through the morning with sprinkles of rain coming and going. However, John and I had made it to the ceremony early enough to stake out a good spot near the fence, and no cold or rain was going to get us to move.

The ceremony that cold morning was fitting of the site itself—quiet and simple. There were some big-name speakers there, but all of them gave modest speeches with all the glory given to those that had lost their lives five years earlier. General Tommy Franks, Pennsylvania Governor Ed Rendell, Congressman Bill Schuster (R-PA), Senator Arlen Specter (R-PA), Senator Rick Santorum, and former Homeland Security Secretary Tom Ridge all spoke at the ceremony.

Four things from this ceremony have stayed with me. First, each speaker made reference to the importance of creating a permanent memorial there. The temporary memorial boasted over 100,000 visitors annually, but the heroes of Flight 93 deserved federal funding for a permanent memorial. Governor Rendell announced that the private side of the fundraising was nearing its goal, and this statement met with a loud round of applause.

Second, Congressman Schuster addressed the issue that I had been contemplating for the past five years. He said that he could think of 535 people who owed their lives to these passengers, referring to the 435 members of the House and 100 Senators. I instantly thought of 30 more—the Senate pages. This was the closest I came to tears that day, but I think it turned out that it was too cold to cry! The congressman thanked these heroes for his own life, and I echoed him in my own thoughts.

Third, the ringing of the bells and the reading of the names made for a powerful moment. This was the culmination of the ceremony and recognized each of the individual passengers in a beautiful way. As the bell tolled after the reading of the name Todd Beamer and for every other passenger, John and I stood with our heads down in prayer. I had craned my neck earlier in the ceremony, looking for Todd's wife, but I never saw her. Surely, her husband was there in spirit, though, and that felt good.

Finally, Senator Specter had the most powerful words, and he provided the moment that I remember best from that ceremony. He didn't do so in his own words, but with a very apt reference to President Lincoln and Gettysburg. Specter referred to a basic message in Lincoln's now-famous address on the battlefield of Gettysburg. Lincoln stated that the actions of the people on the battlefield will be remembered long after the words of the day are forgotten. Of course, Lincoln's words have been remembered quite well, but Specter's point was made. None of the politicians present was an Abe Lincoln, but the truth remains that while the politicians' words could only comfort us for a few moments, the heroics on Flight 93 will live on forever.

While the ceremony was wonderful and the speakers were impressive, the first few minutes of quiet reflection looking out over this special field in Pennsylvania did what needed to be done. I found the closure I needed by simply thanking those 40 passengers at the place of their final rest. I answered the calling of that hallowed ground by paying my respects to my heroes five years after they sacrificed their lives for my friends and me. My generation's challenge will not be complete until we finish the mission started so valiantly by average Americans over the skies of Pennsylvania.

Afterword
A Generation's Challenge

The lessons of 9/11 and the realization of the true nature of the latest enemies of freedom have provided a new generation of Americans with a great challenge. Our objective is clear, yet the road ahead will be difficult. The sacrifices made by this generation in completing this task will be great, but the costs of inaction or weakness would be unimaginable.

Previous generations have faced struggles equally as daunting in their difficulty. President Washington and the other Founding Fathers fought the war for independence and began the democracy that we benefit from today. They made mistakes along the way on the battlefield, in the Articles of Confederation, and on the issue of slavery. A couple of generations later, President Lincoln would have to wage a civil war to preserve the union created by the U.S. Constitution and wipe out the barbaric institution of slavery. Washington and Lincoln laid the foundation for democracy to gain strength as the great battles of the 20th century awaited.

President Wilson reluctantly entered the "war to end all wars." World War I would show the rising power of a resolved American people, but the peace that followed proved to be untenable with Nazis rising to power in Germany. It would take the "greatest generation" to win World War II, and it would take the patient resolve of every president from Truman to Reagan for democratic ideals to defeat the inherently flawed communism of the Soviet Union.

Each of these generations knew that they could not just shrink from the problems of their day. The existence of our nation as we knew it was at stake in each case, and the citizenry understood that it was worth the fight. Each generation left a quality of life to their children that topped their own. The children of these heroic generations went on to strengthen the nation further by becoming inventors, doctors, entrepreneurs, and teachers while living out the American dream preserved for them by their parents and grandparents.

Now America is at its highest point yet. After gaining independence, preserving its own union, winning the hot and cold wars of the 20th century, and winning the war of ideas in the name of democracy, America stands as the brightest beacon of hope to the world. Some would try to block the light of this hope from spreading for fear of losing power over their own oppressed people. Some would even try to fight back against the idea of freedom being an inalienable right of all of humanity by lashing out against the West in general and America in particular. America has entered the 21st century stronger than it has ever been, and the world has followed by democratizing and realizing the prosperity that comes with freedom, but our future success is not inevitable.

America calls on the current generation to defend her from those who would do her harm. Evil regimes that scoff at the concept of liberty while seeking weapons of mass murder stand on one side of the battlefield. They are flanked by a network of radical terrorist groups that do not mind suicidal tactics but invite them as a way to martyrdom. America's side of the battlefield has superior military and economic might, as well as sympathetic allies who know the righteousness of liberty's cause. Unfortunately, these two armies will not meet face to face in an open field of battle where the rules of warfare are clear.

The rogue regimes will defy the world by seeking weapons that level the playing field militarily and can be used to hold the rest of the world hostage. Their terrorist allies will wage their jihad against innocent civilians and use the tactic of terror to attempt political change. Some countries that would like to see America falter on the world stage will balk at opportunities to help fight this important struggle against terror, and we will quickly learn who our true allies are. The end result could be the loss of the population and the economic infrastructure of an entire city in one day.

This is the nature of the challenge this generation faces. Our objective is twofold. First, we must prevent this axis of evil from obtaining such weapons and carrying out such plots. Second, we must put an end to the use of terrorism for political change by promoting democratic ideals such as free and fair elections as the only legitimate way to change government policy. The task is daunting and the obstacles are numerous, but Americans have risen to every epic challenge in the past, and there is no reason to think this generation can't do the same.

We will see the advent of a new Middle East. It has already started in Iraq and Afghanistan. We can see the importance of our success by looking at the reaction of our opponents. The fierce resistance of the terrorists, coupled with the radical ambitions of Iran, has proven that they see these areas as critical to the survival of their evil plans. An unwavering resolve and an understanding of the costs of weakness will be the best weapons we take into this front of the War on Terror.

We will strengthen the interdependence of the world economy to force China and Russia into being stakeholders in our victory. If we are attacked and our economy suffers, they should suffer too—big time. China especially holds the key in solving the nuclear stand-off with North Korea. We will use these quasi-allies when we can to promote our objectives and bring them further into the world community, where democracy will eventually prevail.

We will help Africa to better see the light that shines from the West where stable, democratic governments prosper. There is no longer any excuse for an entire continent to suffer from civil war, health crises, and corrupt governments. Valuing every human life calls on us to help the people of this continent rise out of the third world, and our commitment to winning the War on Terror requires us to recruit them to the side of freedom before our enemies make Africa a new base of operations.

Our own hemisphere presents its own challenges as illegal immigration on our borders poses national security threats and troublesome leaders like Hugo Chavez in Venezuela cozy up to the Iranian regime. We can see that this struggle is truly worldwide and that the consequences are amazingly far-reaching. Our generation should welcome the grand stage of this challenge and seize the opportunity to win a great victory for humanity through the defeat of terror.

The struggles of the 18th century provided for the founding of a noble experiment in our nation. Battles won and innovations made in the 19th century preserved and strengthened our great republic. The 20th century created and preserved liberty in the West against the ideological threats of Nazism, fascism, and communism. The 21st century could create liberty across the entire world, and this generation could do what has become a great tradition of past Americans. We could leave the world and our own children better off because we found the strength to stand up against evil.

May God bless those first brave citizens who took up this fight on September 11, 2001, and may God continue to bless the United States of America.

Acknowledgments

I would like to thank those that helped me take this book from an interesting idea into a reality. My family was behind me from the beginning, and I could feel their love and support throughout the writing process. My friends from high school, the Senate Page school, and the University of Notre Dame also showed their support in ways I will never forget.

I would like to thank my editor, Jennifer Widman, for her help in refining my writing. I would also like to thank all those at Pine Hill Press for being so easy to work with throughout the publishing process. A big thank you goes to Argus Leader columnist David Kranz for all of his friendly advice at the outset of this project and during the writing.

A final thank you goes to my old boss, Senator Tom Daschle, for taking the time to write an introduction for the story of a Senate page.